# 1,001
# Gardening
# Tips & Tricks

## Timeless Advice for Growing Vegetables, Flowers, Shrubs, and More

*Mary Rose Quigg*

Skyhorse Publishing

Skyhorse Publishing books may be purchased in bulk at special discounts for sales promotion, corporate gifts, fund-raising, or educational purposes. Special editions can also be created to specifications. For details, contact the Special Sales Department, Skyhorse Publishing, 307 West 36th Street, 11th Floor, New York, NY 10018 or info@skyhorsepublishing.com.

Skyhorse® and Skyhorse Publishing® are registered trademarks of Skyhorse Publishing, Inc.®, a Delaware corporation.

Visit our website at www.skyhorsepublishing.com.

10 9 8 7 6 5 4 3

Library of Congress Cataloging-in-Publication Data is available on file.

Cover design by Daniel Brount
Cover image by Shutterstock

Print ISBN: 978-1-5107-6223-7
Ebook ISBN: 978-1-5107-6410-1

Printed in China

I would like to dedicate this book to my husband, Joe, as he is the real gardener around our house. My thanks to Karen, Arleen, Orla, Cathal, and Brenda for their encouragement and support.

# Contents

# Introduction

*"There is a great pleasure in working in the soil,
apart from the ownership of it.
The man who has planted a garden feels that
he has done something for the good of the world."
—Unknown*

Gardening for some is a way of life, and for others is a nice hobby to keep them occupied. Regardless of the purpose of your garden, this collection of valuable hints and tips should help to make day-to-day tasks easier.

In this environmentally friendly age it is important to use natural products when appropriate, which you'll find is a theme throughout this book.

All aspects of gardening are covered, from flowers and house-plants to planting shrubs, vegetables, herbs, and trees. The garden pests and tools chapters give very useful tips while healthy gardening should assist in avoiding all those aches and pains. The poems and proverbs included always give me great delight and I hope they make the book more enjoyable.

I have had great pleasure in compiling this practical book from hints and tips that I have acquired over the years. I hope that there is something of interest for you in it and that you find it helpful, interesting, and entertaining. Most of all let it be useful to you in the pursuit of a perfect garden.

—MARY ROSE QUIGG

# Say It with Flowers

*"In joy or sadness, flowers are our constant friends."*
*—Kazuko Okakura*

## LEGENDS & LORE

Some species of flowers are considered unlucky in many parts of the world, particularly when brought into the house.

. . . .

In the UK, honeysuckle, if brought into the house, brought bad luck in Wales but foretold a wedding in Somerset, England.

. . . .

The wild foxglove is a fairy plant in folk tradition. The Irish believe that foxgloves in the house are unlucky. It should never be taken aboard a ship. To pick the foxglove offends the fairies that live within the flowers and will bring bad luck, even death, to the picker and his family. Foxgloves are very poisonous.

. . . .

In the west of England, if snowdrops are brought into the house before the first chickens are hatched, all the eggs will be addled.

. . . .

In Surrey, to take the first primrose into the house meant sickness and sorrow.

. . . .

In Norfolk, lilac was considered unlucky.

. . . .

In the last century in England, a bunch of violets worn around the neck or in the lapel protected against drunkenness.

• • • •

Red and white flowers in the same vase were unlucky, and even today some nurses will not have these flowers in the same vase on a ward.

• • • •

Blue and orange flowers were welcome in homes and hospitals as these colors calm the nerves.

• • • •

The name "iris" is the Greek word for rainbow.
They were planted on women's graves.

• • • •

Lavender has a long reputation as an anaphrodisiac, although some say lavender's relaxing properties may increase sexual desire.

• • • •

*"I think the sweet pea is a frivolous flower
and leads a butterfly's life,
it wanders anywhere, and clings to anything,
and has not any definite aim or ideal."
—Helen Milman*

The rose is known as the queen of flowers. The white rose represents simplicity or happy love; the white rose is for innocence and purity; the yellow rose means perfect achievement and sometimes jealousy; and the red rose signifies passion and sensual desire or shame and occasionally blood and sacrifice.

## CUT FLOWERS

Pick garden flowers in the cool of the morning or in the evening. If it has been raining and the flowers are wet, shake them gently to remove the excess water.

. . . .

Choose half-open blooms or buds with a little color showing. If picked too tightly in bud, they may never open. This is especially true of tulips and roses.

. . . .

The green pointed sepals around the base of the rose should be starting to turn downward. Irises and daffodils should be half open.

. . . .

Gladioli should be picked when the bottom three or four florets are open and the top florets are still in bud.

. . . .

Carnations, dahlias, marigolds, hydrangeas, camellias, and chrysanthemums should be picked when they are fully opened.

. . . .

Take a bucket of warm water into the garden when cutting flowers. Use a sharp pair of pruning clippers and cut the flower stems at an angle—a slanted cut allows a better intake of water.

. . . .

Remove all foliage from the lower portion of the stems standing under the waterline as foliage left on stems below the waterline will rot and pollute the water. Place the flowers immediately in the water.

. . . .

Never overcrowd flowers. Allow enough air to circulate between each flower. Too many flowers crowded together in a bucket may cause the petals to become squashed and bruised. Place the bucket in a cool, dark place and allow the flowers to have a long drink before being arranged.

. . . .

If purchased, flowers cannot be placed in water for several hours; the best way to keep them fresh is to place them in a strong plastic bag with some water in the bottom. Secure the bag with a rubber band. Another method is to wrap flowers in damp newspaper. If traveling by car, place the flowers in the coolest spot.

*"Flowers leave some of their fragrance in the hand that bestows them."*
*—Chinese proverb*

Flowers with woody stems such as roses or chrysanthemums should have the ends of the stems crushed with a heavy object, or slit the stems 1" (2.5 cm) up before arranging.

· · · ·

Before putting the flowers in water, snip off the end of each stem. When flowers are first cut, the sap in the stalk congeals and seals the cut end, preventing it from absorbing water.

· · · ·

When buying cut flowers such as chrysanthemums or daisy types, always look at their center. Green is freshly cut and yellow means they have been cut for some time.

· · · ·

If roses are wilting, cut ½" off the stem, wrap in paper, plunge stems into boiling water for approximately ten seconds, then put into a vase filled with cold water.

· · · ·

Roses can often be perked up by floating the whole stem, head and all, in warm water for half an hour.

· · · ·

Extend the life of carnations by keeping them in a cool place. Add a dash of soda water and a pinch of sugar to the water.

· · · ·

Spiky flowers like lupins or gladioli should have the top three or four buds removed to prevent the head of the spike bending over and to let the remaining buds open properly.

· · · ·

*"Flowers in a city are like lipstick on a woman—it just makes you look better to have a little color."*
*—Lady Bird Johnson*

Foliage and ferns should be submerged in a bath of cold water for several hours before arranging.

. . . .

To revive drooping tulips or roses, wrap tightly in newspaper and put up to their necks in water as hot as the hand can bear and leave until the water cools.

. . . .

To prevent tulips from drooping too quickly after purchase, put pinpricks in the stem just below the flower head.

. . . .

To prevent tulips from drooping, add a pinch of starch to the water. Or place a copper coin in the bottom of the vase.

. . . .

To revive drooping flowers, add an aspirin to every pint of water used in the vase.

. . . .

Singe the stems of poppies over a naked candle flame to make them last longer.

. . . .

Never arrange daffodils and irises in the same vase.

. . . .

Cut the stems of daffodils above the white part, as only the green part of the stem can take up water, and place in very cold water in a cool place for an hour.

. . . .

Daffodils and narcissus have a thick sap oozing from the end of the stems when they are cut. Wipe it off before placing the stems in water. Keep these flowers separate from other flowers when they are being conditioned as the sap can affect other flowers. Stand the stems in 3" (7.5 cm) of water for at least six hours before arranging.

. . . .

Bulb flowers prefer shallow water. If daffodils or narcissus are placed in deep water, the thick stems can become waterlogged, the stems shrivel up, and the petals go papery.

. . . .

Don't place flowers in direct sunlight, over radiators, or on top of television sets. Keep in a well-ventilated part of the room.

. . . .

Prolong the life of fresh flowers in a warm room by adding a few ice cubes to the water twice a day.

. . . .

When changing the water in a vase of fresh flowers, cut off ¼" (5 mm) from the stems before returning to the vase of fresh water.

. . . .

*"Will is the root, knowledge is the stem and leaves and feeling is the flower."*
*—Sterling*

A flower preservative helps destroy bacteria in the water. If a preservative is not used, the water needs to be changed and the stems cut on an angle daily. If a preservative is used, the stems do not require cutting and water needs changing only about twice a week.

. . . .

Flowers like freesias and spray carnations have lots of buds. By using a preservative in the water, it helps develop the buds to open.

. . . .

Add a small piece of charcoal to the water in a vase to keep it odorless. A few drops of bleach added to the water prevents the water from becoming stagnant and does not harm the flowers.

. . . .

Don't place flowers near fruit, as fruit gives off a gas that prematurely ages flowers.

. . . .

Remove dead flowers as these give off gases that affect the others.

. . . .

Unscented flowers last longer.

. . . .

Remove lily stamens as soon as the bloom is sufficiently open as the pollen can damage fabric and polished wood surfaces.

. . . .

If the flower head is too heavy and the stem is hollow, put a thin garden cane or straw inside the stem to support the bloom.

## FLOWER BOXES

Flower boxes are available in a variety of materials including wood, plastic, metal, and terra-cotta. Wooden flower boxes provide better insulation than plastic or metal, with cedar being the best as it is the most resistant to rot. Pine is much less expensive but should be treated. Avoid using commercial wood preservatives, especially creosote.

. . . .

For window boxes, construct a wooden container to fit the windowsill, line it with a plastic sheet, and make a few drainage holes inside. Fill it with pots of plants rather than planting directly into the box. This will make it easier to change planting arrangements if required.

. . . .

Make sure the pots put into the box and the box itself have drainage holes, or the plants will become waterlogged.

. . . .

If plants are to be placed directly into the window box, the box should be at least 8" (20 cm) deep to allow for root growth and to prevent the soil from drying out too quickly.

. . . .

Line boxes well with newspaper to help stop the soil from drying out.

. . . .

In summer the box will need watering every day, so aim to keep the soil moist but never waterlogged.

. . . .

Choose low-growing plants if you want maximum light from your window. Climbers are another option, as they can be trained against the wall around the window.

. . . .

If the box is sited in an exposed position on a wall or balcony, fix it with brackets or strong wire, as strong winds can damage unsecured boxes, leaving them in a dangerous position.

. . . .

Prick over the soil surface of tubs or containers holding long-term plants. This will break up the hard crust and allow easier penetration of water, air, and nutrients.

. . . .

Sprinkle gravel over the soil in window boxes and hanging baskets. This will prevent windows being splashed with mud during heavy showers.

## HANGING BASKETS

Hanging baskets allow for increased gardening in a limited area. By suspending the plant in the air and allowing it to cascade over the sides of the pot, the plant takes on a different quality than if it were growing on the ground.

· · · ·

When using a wire basket or other container with open sides, it is best to line it with damp sphagnum moss before filling it with soil. This not only gives the basket a neat appearance, it also prevents the soil from falling through the large openings. A well-drained soil should be used, such as a mixture of two parts peat, one part sand, and one part vermiculite.

· · · ·

Line hanging baskets with fir trees' leaves. Cover with black polyethylene before filling with compost. The fir keeps its color and smells pleasant when watered.

· · · ·

Placing a hanging basket directly in front of a window will cause lopsided growth, so it needs to be turned occasionally.

· · · ·

Watering is also important. If you have hanging baskets outside or on a screened patio, you will need to water it frequently because of air movement.

. . . .

A wide variety of plants can be used—trailing plants or plants that produce runners can be mixed with other plants.

. . . .

Put used tea bags in the bottom of hanging baskets before adding compost. They are an excellent fertilizer and retain water. Line flower pots with damp paper when planting to help preserve moisture.

. . . .

Hanging baskets need watering twice a day; to make this easier, consider attaching them to a pulley system, available from most garden centers.

. . . .

Water hanging baskets by putting ice cubes on the top; moisture is slowly released as the ice cubes melt. Ensure these do not touch the plants, as this may cause damage.

. . . .

If soil in hanging baskets becomes too dry, add a squirt of washing-up liquid to the water. This helps the water enter the compost instead of just running off.

# DRIED FLOWERS

Any dried plant material can add to an arrangement, so don't overlook twigs with interesting shapes or edges, even if they're grasses or weeds.

. . . .

Baby's breath, thistles, yarrow, goldenrod, and a few other flowers will dry naturally if hung upside down in a dry, warm area.

. . . .

The flowers should be picked before they are in full bloom, since they will open slightly while drying. Foliage should be removed from the stem.

. . . .

Hang flowers upside down in groups of eight to twelve stems, out of the sun, in an area that is warm, dry, and has good air circulation. Flowers are ready to be used when they are crisp.

. . . .

Many flowers can be preserved with the use of desiccants.

. . . .

Silica gel is the most widely used desiccant because it is easy to work with and dries the flowers quickly.

. . . .

A widely used desiccant is a mixture of two parts borax to one part silver sand or silica gel.

. . . .

Flowers take longer to dry in borax mixtures than in silica gel, and it may be difficult to dry delicate flowers with high water content such as rosebuds.

· · · ·

Flowers may be dried with desiccants when they are in bud, or just prior to full bloom when they are at their peak of color.

· · · ·

Artist pastels may be used to add color to dried flowers. Finely grate the pastels into a dust. Mix dust from various colors to achieve a color similar to the natural flower color. Place the dust in a plastic bag and insert the flower, holding on to the stem. Dust the flower with the pastel and remove it from the bag. Shake off all excess dust.

· · · ·

The flower stem should be cut to 1" (2.5 cm) and a wire stem inserted before the flower is dried.

· · · ·

Use an airtight container to dry flowers. Cover the bottom with 1" (2.5 cm) of desiccant and place the flower, with the wire stem looped below the flower, into the desiccant. Care should be taken when covering the flower with desiccant so that the petals retain their natural position. Gently sift the mixture over the flower using a skewer or fine paintbrush to ensure that the grains go into every crevice. Continue this process, shaking the box occasionally, until the flower is covered with ½" (1.2 cm) of desiccant. Cover the container tightly with an airtight lid and leave in a dry place until the flower has completely dried. The length of time required will depend on the desiccant and the type of flower. Carefully pour off the desiccant and gently shake off all excess. Use a soft brush to remove the finest particles.

• • • •

Another method to preserve flowers and other plant materials is using a microwave oven. Microwave drying takes only a few minutes and the dried material looks fresher and more colorful than obtained by other methods. Flowers should be placed in a supportive substance before placing in the microwave oven so that its natural form is retained. Silica gel, borax mixtures, and expanded clay cat litter all work well. Silica gel, however, is the preferred substance. Use only glass, paper, or special microwave containers in which to hold the flowers and desiccants. Do not cover the container. Always place a small cup of water in the oven before cooking to prevent excessive drying. Cooking times vary, depending on the characteristics of the leaf or flower. After cooking, flowers must be left in the drying agent for several hours, and for some specimens an overnight standing period is recommended.

• • • •

When using a microwave oven, it will be necessary to experiment with length of cooking time and length of time that the dried flowers should remain in the desiccant before removal.

. . . .

Spray dried flowers with hair lacquer to prevent them from drooping.

. . . .

To fluff up dried roses, hold the rose head over a steaming kettle and gently tease out the petals.

. . . .

Foliage such as beech should be preserved in a solution of one part glycerine to two parts very hot water. Split the stems up 2" (5 cm) and stand them in 2" to 3" (5–7 cm) of this solution. Leave them until the leaves become shiny, adding more of the solution if necessary. The time will vary from a few days to several weeks depending on the type and condition of the foliage.

. . . .

An easy method to dry seed pods, berries, grasses, and hydrangea flower heads: remove all the foliage and stand them in a vase with a little water in it. Do not replace the water. They will dry out but still retain their color.

# Houseplant Care & Maintenance

*"Don't throw away the old bucket until you know
whether the new one holds water."*
*—Swedish proverb*

## GARDEN HINTS

Dirty vases shorten the life of cut flowers considerably. Soak vases overnight in bleach to remove bacteria.

. . . .

To remove moss and slime from patios, brush with a solution of one cup of washing soda crystals to every pint of hot water. Be careful not to splash on plants.

. . . .

Use kitty litter or sand to melt ice on your walkways instead of salt. When the ice melts, the salt runs off and can burn the roots of neighboring plants and shrubs, causing problems when they begin growing in spring.

. . . .

An old hot water bottle filled sparingly with foam rubber chips is a handy kneeling pad for long gardening jobs.

. . . .

Save wooden ice cream spatulas, lollipop sticks, or plastic knives to use as garden labels. Write on them with a ballpoint pen or waterproof marker.

. . . .

Make labels from colored plastic bottles and color-code different types of plants. Or cut labels from ice cream cartons or margarine tubs and write on them with a waterproof marker.

. . . .

Plastic plant labels that have been written on using permanent ink can be reused if they are soaked in a 75 percent bleach solution for a couple of weeks. Wash thoroughly before using again. Alternatively, use a pencil to mark labels—these can then be used again by erasing the name.

. . . .

To "age" new garden statues, smear with natural yogurt. Algae will quickly cover the item, making it look older.

. . . .

If you are using wicker baskets outside, give them three coats of yacht varnish to protect them.

## HOUSEPLANTS

Houseplants fall mainly into two categories: foliage plants and flowering plants.

. . . .

Foliage plants can be green leaf, colored, or variegated. Green leaf plants are hardy and generally easy to grow. Rubber plants would be the exception. Colored foliage plants need constant higher temperatures and more humid conditions, which may be difficult to maintain in houses. Variegated leaf plants grow well indoors, though they need to be placed in an area with good light.

. . . .

*"God made rainy days, so gardeners could get the housework done."*
*—Unkown*

Flowering plants will flower year after year if cared for properly, and that includes repotting. Flowering pot plants are garden or greenhouse plants specially grown to flower indoors, mainly during spring and winter. They are purchased when the buds have formed and have a slight showing of color. They can flower for several weeks and do not need any special care other than warmth, watering, and deadheading. Once they have finished flowering they should either be discarded, planted out in a greenhouse border, or, if hardy, planted in the flower garden.

. . . .

Most indoor plants come from tropical or arid regions. Plant selection is important to determine whether a particular plant will only survive or thrive in a chosen indoor location.

. . . .

The eventual height and shape of a plant should also be considered when choosing houseplants.

. . . .

It is important to begin with good quality, healthy, pest-free plants. Check that leaves possess good color for the species, with no brown tips or margins. Watch for insects, mites, and signs of disease.

. . . .

Daily exposure to light of eight to sixteen hours is needed for plants to thrive. A southern exposure indoors provides the greatest light intensity, then western, eastern, and northern. Direct sun is not recommended, but nets or venetian blinds can be used as a filter.

. . . .

Do not leave plants between window glass and curtains during winter nights.

. . . .

Plants with variegated foliage require more light than plants with green foliage. If light is insufficient, variegation may be lost. Flowering plants also require higher light intensity.

. . . .

Symptoms of insufficient light intensity or duration include: weak growth; long, spindly stems; poor color in older leaves; and leaf loss or failure to flower.

. . . .

Instead of leaving your houseplants in the same place, turn them around regularly. It will enable all parts to get their fair share of light and grow into a round and bushy shape.

. . . .

Avoid placing plants near heat sources.

. . . .

Central heating is generally run on a time switch, and rooms can have a fluctuating temperature and low temperatures, which can slow the growth of some delicate plants.

. . . .

Avoid drafts and provide fresh air. Symptoms of cold damage to plants include leaf spots or blotches; downward, curled foliage; slowed growth; and root rot.

. . . .

Excessively high temperatures cause yellowish-green foliage with brown, dry edges or tips and spindly growth. Insect, mite, and disease problems may develop quickly under warm conditions as well.

. . . .

Humidity or moisture in the air is necessary and beneficial to most tropical houseplants. To increase the indoor humidity, lightly spray the plant's foliage with water.

. . . .

Another method of increasing humidity is to place the pots on a wet bed of gravel. Double potting may help. Sink pots in a larger container, then fill in between pots with moistened sphagnum moss.

. . . .

Use warm water with a drop or two of mild detergent added to clean a plant's foliage. Rinse washed leaves with clear water to remove soap film. Plants with hairy foliage should be dusted rather than washed.

. . . .

Polish houseplant leaves with cotton balls soaked in milk.

. . . .

More houseplants are killed from improper watering than from any other single cause. When plants are overwatered, the soil remains saturated and root systems are unable to function properly because of lack of oxygen in the soil. Soil-borne bacteria and fungi invade the roots and eventually destroy the entire root system. The plant may struggle for months before it succumbs.

. . . .

Plants that do not receive enough water become stunted and woody, and the leaves turn yellow and finally fall.

. . . .

Watering frequency depends on the kind and size of pot, soil mix, environmental conditions, and plant species, size, and stage of growth.

. . . .

Soil mixes high in organic materials such as peat retain more water, and plants grown in these mixes will not have to be watered as frequently as plants grown in mixes containing high amounts of sand or vermiculite.

. . . .

High temperature and low humidity will increase the rate of water loss from a plant.

. . . .

Generally, plants should be watered when the soil becomes dry to the touch. However, some plants, such as ferns, need to be watered before the soil becomes dry to the touch. Cacti and succulents can tolerate greater dryness; let the soil become crumbly dry for several days before watering.

. . . .

To determine when a plant needs water, feel the soil mix with your fingertip. If the soil mix is slightly moist, wait another day or two and retest before watering.

. . . .

Another method to determine when to water is to use the weight of the container. A dry container and soil mix will be lightweight compared to one that has just been watered.

. . . .

The two methods of watering are applying water to the top of the soil or watering from the bottom of the container with the use of a saucer or tray.

. . . .

*"He who is born with a silver spoon in his mouth*
*is generally considered a fortunate person*
*but his good fortune is small compared*
*to that of the happy mortal who enters this world*
*with a passion for flowers in his soul."*
*—Celia Thaxter*

Watering constantly from below brings nutrient salts to the soil surface. An excess of these salts may accumulate in the upper soil layer in four to six weeks, and this can result in burning of the upper roots and/or stem.

. . . .

Once a month, water thoroughly by applying enough lukewarm (room temperature) water until it runs out of the bottom of the pot. This leaches out excess fertilizer salts in the soil. It also exchanges the air in the soil mix.

. . . .

Do not allow drainage water to seep back into the soil mix; empty the container of excess water as soon as the pot drains completely.

. . . .

If a plant's soil mix is excessively dry and hard to rewet, try double watering. Water once and then again half an hour later; or place the pot in a bucket filled with water. Remove it from the bucket when the soil surface is moist. Allow the pot to drain after using either of these methods.

. . . .

Do not water plants with softened water, as this may add sodium and chloride to the soil mix and cause plant damage.

. . . .

Most plants thrive well in soil mix that is moderately moist. After watering thoroughly, allow the soil mix to dry to a slightly moist condition before watering again.

. . . .

The most likely cause of older plant leaves drooping is under-watering, whereas the most likely cause of younger plant leaves going yellow is overwatering.

. . . .

Put broken eggshells into a watering can, fill with water, and leave overnight. This will extract the nutrients, making an excellent and cheap plant feed.

. . . .

Save the water from an aquarium each time it is changed and use to water houseplants.

. . . .

Use a plastic funnel to water houseplants so the water goes straight into the soil and not over the leaves.

. . . .

In hot weather, water plants in the evening so that the water will soak in around the roots and not evaporate.

. . . .

Occasionally water azalea plants with a mixture of two tablespoons white vinegar to 1 ltr (2 pts) water. Azaleas like acidic soil.

. . . .

To keep plants watered while you are away for a few days, place one end of a pipe cleaner into the soil by the plant and the other end into some water. The pipe cleaner will gradually draw up the water.

. . . .

During a longer stay away, place a towel in the bottom of the bath and add 1" of water. Place houseplants on top of the towel and they will draw up the water as required.

. . . .

Pots must have drainage holes in the bottom whether they are clay, plastic, or ceramic.

. . . .

New clay pots are porous and allow air movement through the sides of the pot. This allows the soil to dry and provides oxygen to the root system.

. . . .

Plastic and glazed ceramic pots are nonporous and do not allow air movement through the sides; the soil holds moisture longer and therefore does not need to be watered as often as soil in clay pots.

. . . .

Soil can be kept from falling through the drainage holes by placing a piece of newspaper or broken pottery over the hole.

. . . .

*"Successful gardening is doing what has to be done
when it has to be done
the way it ought to be done
whether you want to do it or not."*
—Jerry Baker

Do not put a layer of gravel or pieces of broken clay pots in the bottom of pots with drainage holes as this slows down water movement through a pot rather than aiding it. A small piece of broken clay pot can be placed over the drainage hole to prevent soil from draining through the hole.

. . . .

Containers without drainage holes should have a layer of coarse gravel placed in the bottom to allow a space for excess water.

. . . .

To "double-pot," pot the plant in a container that has a drainage hole. Put several inches of gravel in the base of a larger decorative pot and place the potted plant on it.

. . . .

Used pots can be reused if cleaned thoroughly or heat sterilized. Scrub with a 10 percent solution of chlorine bleach and water, using a stiff brush, or wash pots in the dishwasher.

. . . .

Corks from wine bottles are easily sliced up with an old pair of pruning clippers or used whole to keep the drainage holes clear without adding too much weight to hanging or standing pots. Use them in winter to cover the topsoil of pot plants against frost damage.

. . . .

Houseplants must have a loose, well-drained soil. Packed soils should be loosened from time to time, being sure not to damage the root system. Repot plants in spring when growing conditions are best.

. . . .

Most plants thrive in a mix containing one to two parts potting soil, one to two parts moistened sphagnum peat moss, and one part coarse sand or vermiculite.

. . . .

Soil from the garden can be used in a mix if it is first "pasteurized." The soil should be moistened twenty-four hours prior to heating. Place soil on a baking sheet, 2" (5 cm) deep, and heat in an oven at 180°F for thirty minutes. If soil is high in clay content it does not make the best mix.

. . . .

If after watering a plant most of the water drains out of the pot, then the plant's soil ball is shrinking. This happens when the potting mix is allowed to dry out and pulls away from the sides of the pot. To avoid this, change to a potting mix with less peat moss in it and water more regularly.

. . . .

To correct an existing problem, immerse the entire pot in water to make sure the root ball gets plenty of moisture. If the shrinkage is severe, repot the entire plant.

. . . .

Fertilizer should only be used on healthy, well-watered, and actively growing plants. Use complete water-soluble fertilizers.

. . . .

Dilute fertilizer to about one tenth the recommended label rate and use this solution to water plants at every watering. Once a month, flush pots with clear water to wash out excess salts.

. . . .

Houseplant fertilizer stakes are a continuous feed method as some fertilizer dissolves with each watering over a period of three to twelve months. However, use these with caution since it is not easy to correct a salts problem should it occur. If the plant goes into a dormant phase or if dark and cloudy weather occurs, these fertilizers can't be leached quickly from the soil mix.

. . . .

Most houseplants do not require fertilizer during the winter since there is little rapid growth at this time. Feeding once or twice during the winter months will be adequate for most plants.

. . . .

White discoloration near the top or bottom of pots or a crust of salts at the soil line may indicate that the plant is being overfertilized and/or overwatered. If salts are high and the soil excessively dry, root damage or death is possible.

. . . .

Pinching stimulates new growth from buds lower on the stem. It is commonly using on vining and bushy plants. The growing stem tip is removed, just above a node. Pinch with your thumb and forefinger, or use sharp scissors to make the cut. Mature plants can be pinched to produce dense, bushy growth, especially on fast-growing, soft-stemmed plants with long, lanky stems. Once side shoots form, they can be pinched to promote even more new growth.

. . . .

Repotting should be done only as needed, during spring or summer when the plant is actively growing. Do not repot ailing or dormant plants or those with flower buds or open flowers.

. . . .

A plant needs repotting if roots are growing out of the drainage hole or "surfacing" in the pot, if the plant wilts shortly after watering, or if it requires frequent watering. As roots grow, they compact the soil, decreasing the pore space, which holds water and air for the root system.

. . . .

Choose a pot 1"–2" (2.5–5 cm) larger in diameter. With each 1" (2.5 cm) diameter increase in pot size, the volume of soil nearly doubles.

. . . .

If a plant is repotted into too large a pot, the root system is surrounded by a large volume of soil, which can become excessively moist and slow to dry out, leading to root rot.

. . . .

The plant to be repotted should be slightly moist. Remove it from its pot and gently disturb the root system with your fingers so that roots are headed outward from the root ball. Place some soil mix in the new pot and position the plant so it will be at the same depth; fill in around the sides of the ball with new soil mix. Water well so excess water drains out of the container.

. . . . .

For plants in large containers that are impossible to repot, carefully remove the top two or three inches of soil and replace with fresh soil every two years. This process is known as top dressing.

. . . . .

It is beneficial for some plants to be put outdoors during the summer months, but it is important not to move plants outside until the danger of frost is over.

. . . . .

If the weather is very sunny, then put the plants in a shady area so that they are gradually exposed to the sunlight.

. . . . .

Plants outside will grow rapidly and require frequent fertilization and watering if rainfall is not adequate.

. . . . .

Plants should be carefully inspected for insect or mite pests before bringing them indoors. Control any pests found as indoor conditions may help to increase them rapidly.

. . . . .

Winter is a good time to check houseplants, potted patio plants stored in the garage, and greenhouses for tiny, soft-bodied pests. Get rid of pests by hand or vacuum them off.

. . . .

Remove and destroy plant parts or the entire plant if it is totally infested. Discard infested soil and clean pot or container as well.

. . . .

When using chemical pesticides, note that few pesticides are registered for indoor use on houseplants. Read labels carefully for where and how to use a pesticide. If indoor use is not listed on the label, take the plant to be treated outside, away from children and pet traffic areas. Leave the plant outside a day or two after spraying.

. . . .

Isolate infested plants from others so pests don't spread from plant to plant.

. . . .

Place aluminium foil around the base of a plant to disorient winged pests like aphids and prevent them from landing.

. . . .

Paint a small dish yellow and fill it with water to attract and drown winged aphids.

. . . .

To avoid insect infestation of your houseplants, add a little garlic powder when watering them. Remove greenflies from plants by spraying with soapy water or water infused with garlic. Always test the spray on a small area first in case it damages the plant.

## HOUSEPLANTS FROM FRUIT

Many unusual plants can be grown from the seeds of fruit such as peaches, dates, and avocado.

. . . .

Put peach and date stones in small pots of compost, cover with black polyethylene, and leave to germinate at 64°F/18°C. Peach stones must be kept at 39°F/4°C for a few weeks before planting.

. . . .

For avocados to germinate, insert two or three cocktail sticks or matchsticks into the sides of the stone. Suspend the stone over a jar of water with the pointed end upward. The base of the stone should be just touching the water. It will take six to eight weeks for roots to appear. Plant the stone with the roots down 2"-3" (5-7 cm) deep in compost, in a large pot. Keep in a warm, humid place with plenty of light. After a few weeks, a single shoot will emerge and develop long, slender leaves. Avocado plants will grow rapidly; pinch out the growing shoot when the required height is reached. Repot annually.

. . . .

Seeds of citrus fruit such as lemons, oranges, and grapefruit can produce plants. Plant the seeds as soon as they are removed from the fruit. Fill a 4" (10 cm) pot with compost and water well. Leave to drain. Plant four to six seeds ½" (1 cm) deep. Cover the pot loosely with a polyethylene bag secured with a rubber band. Keep at 64°F/18°C for a few weeks until shoots appear. Remove the bag and keep at the same temperature until the plants are well established. Plant out singly into 4" pots. These plants will grow to 3'-4' (1 m) bushy plants with a lovely smell.

· · · ·

To grow the top of a pineapple into a plant, cut the top of the fruit below the first row of seeds on the skin. Fill a 4" (10 cm) pot up to ¾" (1.9 cm) below the rim with compost. Sprinkle a thin layer of coarse sand on top. Place the pineapple crown on the sand and sprinkle a little more compost over the fleshy part.

· · · ·

Cover the pot with a polyethylene bag and leave in a shaded place at 64°F/18°C for eight weeks. The leaves should look fresh or new leaves will appear. When the plant looks well established, remove the polyethylene bag and repot into a larger pot. The plant can grow to 2' (60 cm).

## GARDEN HINTS

To make brand-new containers look immediately old, coat them
in natural yogurt and leave in the sun.

. . . .

Cut the top and bottom off large plastic bottles to use as sleeve
and arm protectors when pruning or hedging.

. . . .

Give old pottery vases a new look by sanding them lightly and
coating with any color of matte paint.

. . . .

Use an old coffee jar to spread dry fertilizer. Drill holes into the
plastic lid, fill with fertilizer, and shake where required.

. . . .

A natural way of removing flying insects/eggs etc. in
greenhouses is by using a vacuum cleaner.

. . . .

A piece of wood placed upright in a plastic water barrel will
prevent the barrel splitting when it freezes.

. . . .

To reduce the amount of compost in a large plant pot, place a
layer of broken crockery, then broken Styrofoam, to fill large plant
pots to one-third of the depth of the pot.

. . . .

*"You will catch more flies with a spoonful of honey than with a gallon of vinegar."*
*—Unknown*

Reuse chopsticks to stir right to the bottom of watering cans, support young tomato plants, and as a dibber for uprooting seedlings before transplanting.

. . . .

Don't discard your worn-out Wellingtons. Cut off the legs and wear them on your arms when pruning prickly shrubs.

. . . .

To give young vine plants a place to grow upward on, a trellis can be placed about 3 ft (1 m) above the plants and the "string" can be hung from the bottom of the trellis. This gives the vines a way of climbing to the trellis for support.

. . . .

When fixing a trellis to a wall, use batons to raise it from the surface. This allows the air to flow freely around the climbing plant and reduce the problems of mildew and other diseases.

# It's Planting Time

*"All the flowers of all the tomorrows are
in the seeds of today and yesterday."*
—*Chinese proverb*

## GARDEN HINTS

Punch holes in the bottom of old plastic or paper cups and use to
plant seeds.

• • • •

Make a small propagator from an old plastic candy jar. Lay it
horizontally and place a plant tray inside, then replace the lid.

• • • •

Cut the base of clear plastic soft-drink bottles to make a mini
cloche to protect planted-out seedlings from slugs and cold.
Unscrew the tops gradually to acclimatize plants to cooler air.

• • • •

Cut cardboard milk cartons in half horizontally to plant sweet
corn, beans, sweet peas, etc. When planting out, cut the sides
away with scissors to avoid damaging the roots.

• • • •

Plastic cartons that take-out food comes in make excellent seed
trays for standing pots on in cold frames.

• • • •

Cardboard egg cartons are excellent for planting individual seeds, one per hole. When planting out the seedlings, cut the box into its compartments and plant each in the ground; the cardboard is biodegradable and will disintegrate.

. . . .

When sowing fine seeds, mix with sand for easier sowing.

. . . .

Leave cans of water to warm up in a greenhouse to water tender seedlings.

. . . .

Soak seeds in a cup of cool tea, then place into the refrigerator for three days to prepare them for planting.

. . . .

When growing sweet peas from seed, fill a pot two-thirds full with compost and water well, then top up with dry compost. Plant seeds ½" (1 cm) beneath the surface of the compost. This way the seeds will draw up as much water as required and will not rot.

. . . .

To enhance the germination of morning glory or lupin seeds, nick each seed with a pair of nail clippers. Place the seeds on a lightly dampened paper towel, fold the towel over, and place inside a plastic zipper bag for a day or so before planting.

## SEEDS AND TRANSPLANTING

When using pots or trays that have been used previously, disinfect them by scrubbing them in warm soapy water, then rinse well.

. . . .

When planting seeds indoors, it is important to use a sterile medium. Garden soil can be used but it should be sterilized. Since this is a tedious procedure, it is probably better to use a commercially available mix.

. . . .

Once you've added potting soil to your pots, firm the mixture down to ½" (1.2 cm) from the top of the container using a flat piece of wood or the base of another pot.

. . . .

Sow the seeds thinly and evenly. Cover large seeds with ¼" (6 mm) sieved compost, while smaller seeds just need a light dusting of compost. An old coarse flour sieve is ideal for sieving the compost.

. . . .

*"Many things grow in the garden that were never sown there."*
*—Thomas Fuller*

Water the compost by standing the tray or pot in water halfway up its sides. Remove from the water when the compost is well wet.

. . . .

Label the containers and cover with glass, polyethylene, or a clear heavy plastic bag. Individual pots can be placed inside plastic bags closed with a rubber band. This keeps the planting medium both warm and moist.

. . . .

Put trays and pots in a warm, shady place.

. . . .

If moisture forms inside the bag or on the glass, wipe it off.

. . . .

Seeds can take from five days to three weeks to germinate. Most seedlings show a pair of small round or oval leaves.

. . . .

When seedlings sprout, remove the covering. Otherwise, you risk suffocating the young seedlings. Place the tray or pot into a position where there is more light but out of direct sunshine.

. . . .

Seedlings need a lot of light. If they receive insufficient light they become tall and spindly or "leggy."

. . . .

Place near a large window that receives full sun. In dull weather, artificial light should be used as well. Use bulbs recommended for growing plants and place them 12" (30 cm) above the seedlings. If using only artificial lighting, the lights will need to be kept on at least fourteen hours a day. Fluorescent tubes don't produce as much heat, reducing the chance of seedlings drying out quickly.

. . . .

The medium should be kept moist, but not wet or soggy. Water from the base, allowing the medium to soak up the water like a sponge.

. . . .

To prevent seedlings from drying out, it is important to water carefully. If using total artificial lighting it is quite easy to predict how often watering is required. When using a sunny windowsill, it will help if the containers are placed on a raised bed of gravel spread across the bottom of a large pan with a small amount of water. Make sure the water level is below that of the gravel so that the plant containers rest on the gravel and not on the water.

. . . .

"In every failure lies the seeds of success."
—Deepak Chopra

It is important not to start seeds indoors too early. If they outgrow trays or small pots, try thinning them and transplanting the largest to bigger pots, but it is easier to plant them outside just as they become large enough to survive transplanting. This is generally four to six weeks after sowing, when they have at least two sets of true leaves. If aiming to plant in the first week of May, start the seeds around mid-March. Toward the end of this period, you may want to provide your seedlings a little food in the form of a weak, water-soluble fertilizer.

• • • •

As soon as the first true leaf appears from between the seed leaves, the seedlings are ready to be transplanted.

• • • •

When transplanting, fill a seed tray with compost. Mark out planting holes with a dibber or pencil to ensure even spacing. The holes should be spaced over 1" (2.5 cm) apart in each direction. A standard seed tray will accommodate forty to ninety seedlings. Using a plant label or a narrow piece of plastic, lever up a small clump of seedlings. Catch a seedling by one leaf and use the dibber or pencil to tease it away from the clump. Drop the seeding into the prepared hole and firm the compost around it gently with the dibber. When the tray is full of seedlings, label and water with a fine-rose attachment on a watering can. Place the tray in a cold frame or on an indoor window ledge but away from direct sunshine for a few days. Then move into direct sunlight for a few weeks until the plants are well established and healthy.

• • • •

*"Scatter seeds of Happiness, Hope, Kindness, and Love."—Unknown*

Before planting out, the seedlings must be hardened off. Move to an unshaded cold frame or leave them under a covered porch or patio for a few days. Or cover them during nighttime with newspaper or a light sheet.

. . . .

When transferring transplanted seedlings either from a garden nursery or seeds started indoors, make sure the weather conditions are favorable before placing outdoors.

. . . .

Prepare the proper environment before planting out seedlings. Good soil preparation is the single most important thing you can do for your plants. Loosen soil to at least 6" (15 cm), add organic matter (such as peat moss, compost, or manure), and mix well. Rake to level.

. . . .

Plant when the soil is moist; if the weather is dry, then water the soil the day before transplanting.

. . . .

To transplant to the garden, knock the seed tray on the ground to loosen the compost and leave a space to insert a trowel or fingers beneath the compost. Break away a row of plants and gently separate each plant, ensuring there is a good root system. Dig a planting hole with a trowel; make it wide and deep enough to accommodate the plant's root system. Set the plant so that the base of the stem is level with the surface of the soil. Fill the hole and firm down the soil around the plant.

. . . .

Encourage bushy plants by pinching out the growing tip.

· · · ·

The spacing between plants depends on the species of plant. A general rule is to space plants apart half their eventual height, except for plants that spread, which should be spaced full height apart.

· · · ·

Don't smother new plants with too thick a soil blanket.

· · · ·

Nourish young plants well during growth spurts. Water with diluted water-soluble fertilizers or manure tea from a watering can, or side-dress the plants with compost.

· · · ·

Weeds rob seedlings of nutrients, so constant weeding is important to ensure sturdy plants.

· · · ·

Once plants flower, keep the color coming by removing faded flower heads (deadheading).

· · · ·

If a flowering plant blooms and then fades, revitalize it by shearing off the faded blooms and one-third of the top growth, then fertilize. This restores the performance and blooming of "past their prime" plants.

· · · ·

It helps to pinch out the center of young flowering plants, such as petunias and fuchsias, to encourage more bushy side growth. Tall delphiniums, sunflowers, and dahlias may need to be tied to stakes.

. . . .

When moving perennials, it is a good time to acquire more plants. Pull off the side shoots and transplant in a new location where the soil has been loosened and well watered. It is advisable to do this on a cloudy day.

. . . .

When choosing plants from a garden center, always pick healthy stock. Select stocky, deep-green plants with buds slightly showing. Spindly plants in full bloom make poor transplants. Avoid plants with discolored or wilted leaves.

. . . .

When transplanting, select plants that are about as tall as they are wide, dark-green in color, vigorously growing, and free of spots or lesions on the leaves, indicating disease problems.

. . . .

If bedding plant transplants have become root bound (roots are crowded and encircling each other), gently loosen the root ball at planting time.

. . . .

Set the root ball of the transplant into the hole, filling in around it with soil. Leave enough space between seedlings to allow each plant to reach its mature potential without crowding its neighbors.

• • • •

Transplant larger nursery stock the same way you would seedlings. Control invasive plants, such as tansy, mint, or bamboo by planting them in their pots to contain their runners. Just cut the bottom out of the pot before planting.

• • • •

Do not fertilize transplants for several weeks. Instead, water thoroughly, using a splash of B vitamins to help overcome transplant shock. Water regularly until plants show new growth, indicating they're rooting and surviving well.

• • • •

Grow varieties of plants that require little or no staking and plant closely so they support each other.

• • • •

Before planting shrubs in the garden, lay the plants out in their pots roughly in the place where you plan to plant them. This way you'll be able to check if they are in the right places before any heavy work has been done.

• • • •

When bringing delicate plants indoors to protect them from cold weather, put several into the same pot to take up less space.

• • • •

*"Gardens are the result of a collaboration
between art and nature."*
*—Penelope Hobhouse*

If tender buds or shoots become frozen, thaw them out slowly by spraying with cold water before the sun shines. Otherwise they may get scorched.

• • • •

Planting seeds too closely together or overwatering can cause damping-off disease where the base of the seedling turns brown and dies.

## BULBS

When buying bulbs, always select carefully. Good bulbs are plump, firm, and free from blemishes. They should also be a good size (for the type); if they are too small, they may not flower in the first year.

• • • •

Bulbs should be planted in clusters. They look good under a tree, in a tub, or in window boxes.

• • • •

If planting bulbs in grass, remember to choose low-growing varieties. To achieve a random look, scatter the bulbs onto the lawn and plant where they fall. Remember, bulbs planted in lawns make mowing more difficult.

• • • •

Bulbs not planted deep enough do not thrive well. As a general rule, they should be planted at three times the depth of the bulb. If the bulb measures 2" (5 cm) from top to bottom, they should be planted 6" (15 cm) deep.

. . . .

When the flowers are finished, the dead flower heads should be cut off before they turn to seed to prevent the plant being weakened for the next year. Leave the stems to turn brown and die off naturally. This will allow nourishment to be returned to the bulb for next year's flowers. Don't trim the leaves off or tie them down.

. . . .

If you need to remove the bulbs to make way for other planting, carefully lift out the bulbs and replant them in a corner of your garden with wire netting beneath them. Lift and replant in autumn.

. . . .

Daffodil bulbs should be in before the end of October. Small varieties developed from wild daffodils should be planted in holes 3" (7 cm) deep, other varieties at 6" (15 cm) deep.

. . . .

Tulips can be planted from October until the end of November in holes about 4" (10 cm) deep.

. . . .

Don't plant tulips in the same spot two consecutive years. Never plant tulips and lilies together, as they suffer from the same diseases.

. . . .

After tulips flower, pull away leaves as soon as they are yellow and withered to prevent disease entering the bulbs. Apply a liquid fertilizer to build the bulbs up so they'll be ready for next season. Feed once a week for a month.

. . . .

Snowdrops can be planted as bulbs before the end of September in holes 3"–4" (7–10 cm) deep. If possible, plant them immediately after flowering while still in leaf.

. . . .

To give bulbs a boost, apply a light feed of a general fertilizer once they have flowered and the leaves have started to die down.

. . . .

Crocuses should be planted before the end of September at about 2"–3" (5–7 cm) deep.

. . . .

*"Advice on dandelions: If you can't beat them, eat them."—Unknown*

When planting bulbs indoors for Christmas flowering, buy "prepared" bulbs as these have been treated to speed up their development. The middle of September is generally considered to be the best time for planting to ensure flowers for Christmas. Put some well-soaked bulb fiber or potting compost into a pot, leaving enough space to allow the bulbs to be placed inside with the tips just below the rim of the container. They should be placed close together but not touching. Cover with bulb fiber or compost and water well. The container should then be placed in a cool spot—in a shed, or bury it in a shady corner of the garden. Darkness is not necessary but coolness is. Do not put it in a black plastic sack as this encourages mold.

• • • •

After ten to twelve weeks, young green shoots should appear (these will be paler if the pot has been kept in the dark). When the shoots have reached about 2" (5 cm) in height, bring the pot into a cool room and they should flower in time for Christmas.

• • • •

Plant bulbs in the garden in a buried flowerpot. This can then be easily lifted when bulbs have finished flowering.

• • • •

When storing bulbs over the winter, make sure to separate them into different colors and label the boxes to make it easier for planting arrangement in the spring.

# LEGENDS & LORE

Clover was one of the first plants cultivated by man and has been highly regarded since ancient times. The three-leaf shamrock is associated with the Christian Trinity and is the national emblem of Ireland. The rare four-leaf clover is also a Christian symbol with its four leaves representing the cross. Some claim the four-leaf clover wards off evil. Each leaf represents different aspects of happiness: one leaf for fame, the second wealth, the third a faithful lover, and the fourth excellent health. Wearing a four-leaf clover in your shoe will bring you a mate. Four-leafed clovers are well known for their luck and magical charm, but according to an old wives' tale they are not *found*; they *make themselves known* only to lucky people.

· · · ·

According to Christian legend, the daisy sprung from Mary's tears during the flight into Egypt. It has always been associated with purity, innocence, and loyal love. According to German folklore, daisies picked between noon and 1 p.m. have magical qualities. They should be dried and carried as a good luck charm.

· · · ·

The name of the dandelion comes from the French term for a lion's tooth (*dent-de-lion*). To carry your thoughts to your sweetheart, blow the feathered seeds off the puffball. To dream of a dandelion is supposed to be bad luck.

· · · ·

Ivy is a lucky plant. If it grows on a house, it protects those within from witchcraft and evil. In Christmas decorations it is as lucky to the woman as holly is to the man, and therefore should never be omitted if all the family are to share alike in the blessings of the season. The wood of the plant was supposed to have the power of separating water from wine when these were mixed together. The leaves, roots, and wood of ivy were used in a number of folk-remedies, some practical and some mainly magical.

· · · ·

In Greek burials, it was the custom to cover a dead body with violets as a symbol of both the beauty and the transitory nature of life. In literature, violets are often associated with modesty and simplicity.

# The Outdoor Garden

*"Though a tree grows so high,*
*the falling leaves return to the root."*
*—Malaysian Proverb*

A soil test is the most efficient and money-saving step toward better gardening. A soil test measures levels of nutrients (nitrogen, phosphorus, and potassium) that are available for plants, as well as what your soil lacks.

• • • •

The test also indicates your soil's pH level—the relative acidity or alkalinity—that affects how plants take up nutrients and thrive. Soil pH ranges from 1.0 (acid) to 14.0 (highly alkaline), with 7 being neutral. In certain areas, soil is typically more acid (in rainy areas) or more alkaline (in dry areas) and needs to be amended accordingly for plants to thrive there. To raise too-low pH (acidic) soil: add lime, dolomite limestone, or wood ashes. To lower too-high pH (alkaline) soil: add horticultural sulphur, composted oak leaves, or pine needles.

• • • •

Check the pH of garden soil before planting expensive or unusual shrubs and perennials. Many plants thrive in any soil, but there are some that dislike acidic soil. Use a simple pH testing kit to determine what plants are suitable in your garden.

• • • •

Never add lime to soil without first checking its pH to ascertain if it is required.

• • • •

Never apply manure and lime to soil at the same time. They will react together and produce harmful ammonia. Allow at least two months between applications of lime and manure.

• • • •

To determine the texture of soil, rub some soil between moistened fingers. A sandy soil feels rough, a clay soil feels greasy, and a loam soil somewhere in between.

• • • •

When digging soil in the autumn, don't break down the clods as the winter rain will make them compacted. Leave the clods rough and they will disintegrate slowly.

• • • •

Improve clay soil by double digging and incorporating plenty of organic matter as you work it.

• • • •

Use manure within a year, as a large proportion of the nutrients will be leached out after that.

## FLOWERS AND SHRUBS

Keep deadheading flowers and they will keep blooming for much longer, instead of producing seeds early in the season.

. . . .

To trap aphids, put some water and oil in a yellow dish and set it in the garden; they love the color yellow and when they land on the water, the oil will prevent them from escaping.

. . . .

Plant garlic or parsley under rose plants to keep aphids away.

. . . .

Pinch off the tendrils of sweet peas to improve their flowering capacity.

. . . .

Bury fuchsias in the winter to protect them from the frost.

. . . .

Use toilet paper rolls to plant sweet peas, runner beans, or garden peas as they need a good root run.

. . . .

To deepen the color of your blue hydrangea, simply grow the plant with iron nails around its base. This alters the pH balance of the soil, which then changes the color of the flower itself.

. . . .

*"Should I weed the lawn, or say it's a garden?"*
*—Unknown*

Do not deadhead hydrangea as they give protection for next year's buds. Prune when the danger of frost is past.

• • • •

When repotting or moving prickly plants or conifers, cut the bottom off an old compost bag to form a tube which you can then place over the plant. Tie the top and bottom with string. This will condense any awkward branches and also protect your arms.

• • • •

A circle of twigs 20" (50 cm) high provides a better support for border plants than a single stake, and is less obtrusive.

• • • •

Do not clear away old vegetation or foliage around plants in borders, as this gives protection in severe weather.

• • • •

When planting up summer annuals in pots or baskets, plant up half a dozen extra pots in ordinary flower pots and nurture them in the same way. As the summer progresses and bare areas appear where plants have either died or perennials haven't survived the winter, simply position the pots in the gaps and fill the borders instantly.

• • • •

To help when repotting plants into larger pots, place the current pot into the larger pot and push compost firmly into the gap between the two. Gently remove the inner pot to leave the correct size hole into which the plant can be dropped.

. . . .

To prevent slugs getting to plants in containers, smear the outside of the container with petroleum jelly or WD40.

. . . .

When planting grown container plants, disturb the roots as little as possible so that they continue to benefit from the compost they are grown in. Water as usual after planting.

. . . .

When planting new climbers and ramblers for the spring, plant them about a foot from the supporting wall and lead them to the wall via a cane. This will give the roots room to develop properly and help to give years of healthy growth.

. . . .

Use old tights or stockings cut into strips to tie up plants, rather than twine, which can slice into stems.

. . . .

Do not remove dead leaves from plants damaged by frost as they are nature's way of protecting new young shoots.

. . . .

*"A weed is a plant that has mastered every survival skill except for learning how to grow in rows."*
*—Doug Larson*

Never move or plant anything if the ground is frozen. Wait until the soil warms up.

• • • •

To kill grass or weeds growing around low carpeting plants, make up a mixture of grass weed killer as directed on the container. Add a squirt of liquid dish soap. Put on a pair of strong rubber gloves and then a knitted mitten or thick sock. Dip your hand into the mixture and let the sock or mitten soak. Squeeze out the excess and then touch the weeds or grass. The slimy solution will stick to the weeds and not destroy the plants.

## OUTDOOR PLANT CONTAINERS

Choosing a container for plants is important. Plastic pots are cheap, light, and durable and they keep the soil moist; however, they can turn brittle and crack.

• • • •

Terra-cotta pots are made from baked clay and are very attractive; however, they are heavy, break easily, and are subject to frost damage.

• • • •

Glass fiber containers have a wide variety of molds and colors. They can look like stone but are much lighter. They are strong, durable, and repairable, but are expensive.

. . . .

Reconstituted stone pots are crushed stone molded into shape. Imitation classical urns and vases are very attractive but extremely heavy and should be used with caution in roof gardens or balconies.

. . . .

If using new concrete plant containers, leave them outdoors for a few weeks to weather fully, as some concrete can contain setting agents that may be harmful to plants.

. . . .

Wooden half barrels are useful plant containers. Line the barrels with strong plastic to stop the compost from coming in contact with the wood. Make drainage holes both in the plastic and the barrel.

. . . .

When using heavy plant containers, make sure to position them in their intended final sites before filling, as they are difficult to move. If they do have to be moved, put lengths of old scaffolding pipes under the pot to use as rollers.

. . . .

Take the wheels off old suitcases, shopping carts, or old strollers and fix them to the bottom of heavy patio pots. This will allow them to be easily moved around the garden or pathways.

. . . .

*"A tree is known by its fruit; a man by his deeds.*
*A good deed is never lost;*
*he who sows courtesy reaps friendship,*
*and he who plants kindness gathers love."*
*—Basil*

To reduce the weight of compost in a large pot, fill the container with empty plastic bottles to a depth of 8" (12 cm). Cover with a layer of polyethylene, making holes in it for drainage. Fill to the top with compost.

. . . .

When stacking terra-cotta pots, place a few sheets of newspaper between them to prevent the pots from jamming together and making them difficult to separate.

## LAWNS

The most important ingredient in a good lawn is the preparation of the ground before sowing or laying turves. Good drainage is essential, though the soil itself must be moisture retentive. For the grass to become established, the lawn must be properly fertilized, watered regularly in dry weather, and weeds eliminated.

. . . .

A lawn can be sown or laid at any time of the year when the weather isn't frosty or dry. The best months are April and September.

. . . .

When choosing turf for the lawn, make sure that it is free from coarse grass and weeds, as these are difficult to eradicate.

. . . .

The thickness of the turves is no guide to its quality. Generally thin turves properly laid root more rapidly than thick ones. All turves purchased should be of equal thickness.

. . . .

Lawn turves are delivered in rolls. Since these are heavy to move, they should be dropped as close as possible to where they are required.

. . . .

Lay the turves as soon as possible after delivery, as the grass tends to yellow after five days, depending on the weather.

. . . .

Use an old tenon saw to cut the turf to size and shape. This is a much safer way to cut the turf than using a knife that could slip and injure the person using it.

. . . .

When laying the turf, avoid placing a short piece at the end of a row where it will fray. Move a large piece to the end and put the smaller piece next to it.

. . . .

Stand on a wooden plank when working with lawn turves to avoid damaging them.

. . . .

When the area has been completely turfed, roll it twice, the second time at right angles to the first. Do not roll again until the turf has rooted, and then only lightly.

. . . .

To prevent cracks or shrinkage, water newly laid turf once or twice a week with a garden sprinkler.

. . . .

If cracks appear in a lawn after laying or during the summer months, they can be filled with a fifty-fifty mixture of sand and non-soil compost or peat. Reseed at the same time. Repeat procedure when necessary.

. . . .

In the springtime, replace any patches of turf that have failed to root, or seed these areas when the weather is right.

. . . .

When seeding a lawn, choose a calm day. The surface of the soil should be dry, but it should be moist underneath. To ensure even coverage, sow half the seed across the area and the remainder up and down.

. . . .

After sowing a lawn, lightly rake in the seed to avoid exposure on the surface and it will germinate better. Do not roll.

. . . .

Do not walk on the lawn when the grass is frozen. The grass blades will break and leave brown marks until the spring.

• • • •

Repair bad patches of lawn with surplus pieces of turf acquired when making new flower beds, etc. Cut to size and fit into the gap. Add plenty of compost into the cracks and water well.

• • • •

To kill toadstools or fungi on the lawn, water with diluted Jeyes Fluid. It doesn't damage the grass.

• • • •

The lawn should be fed in the springtime to encourage grass growth. A good time to use lawn feed is when it is raining lightly. The rain prevents the feed from scorching the grass.

• • • •

Regular mowing is important. When the growth is most vigorous in late spring, the lawn should be mown frequently. This encourages thicker grass cover, which will help to reduce weed and moss growth.

• • • •

Do not mow grass when it is very wet. Avoid cutting very close. Grass should be left slightly longer in dry weather and in spring and autumn.

## GARDEN HINTS

Apply a teaspoon of salt directly onto a weed such as dandelion in your lawn to kill it.

. . . .

Avoid splashing creosote on plants when treating woodwork as it can cause severe leaf scorching.

. . . .

The secret of getting a new ivy to cling to your walls is to cut it hard back after planting. New shoots get a grip straightaway—old ones never do.

. . . .

Hang nets under trees in the autumn to catch some of the falling leaves and save having to rake them off the ground.

. . . .

When raking leaves in the garden, sweep them into a pile and water lightly with a watering can. Soggy leaves will not fly away in the wind and more will fit into the wheelbarrow or sack.

. . . .

When gathering rubbish in the garden or house, roll a piece of cardboard into a tube and place it in a garbage bag. The cardboard must be able to expand when released in the liner so that it can stand on the ground unaided. This will enable you to have both hands free when loading the bag with rubbish. As you fill the bag, raise the cardboard slightly until the bag is full. Remove the cardboard, which can be used again, and tie the liner as usual.

. . . .

*"To forget how to dig the earth and to tend the soil
is to forget ourselves."—Mahatma Gandhi*

When carrying heavy loads, such as compost, in the wheelbarrow, always load more at the front of the barrow (over the wheel). That way the barrow will move better and not make your arms painful.

. . . .

Use an empty, cut-off lemonade bottle to water your growing bags. Turn the bottle upside down in the growing bag and pour the water directly into the funnel that the bottle makes. The water will run directly into the growing bag and not leak out onto the floor.

## PONDS

When building a new pond, remember that siting it in full sun will encourage the growth of algae, so position it in a lightly shaded area.

. . . .

When the hole has been dug for a pond, use whole newspapers soaked in water to line it instead of using sand. The papers can be molded around any contour. Or use old carpet. Both will protect the liner for many years.

. . . .

Do not line a pond with normal polyethylene sheeting, as it will tear easily. Use purpose-made butyl rubber sheeting, which should carry a guarantee against leaking.

. . . .

Install an overflow pipe in a new pool, as heavy rainfall could cause the water to spill over the edge.

. . . .

Take a pair of old tights, cut the legs off, and place one leg inside the other. Fill the tights with aquatic compost and tie off the open end. To plant, burn a hole in the tights with a match at various points, and plant your aquatic or marginal plants through the holes. Locate the bag around the edge of the pond to suit requirements. The plants will soon grow through the tights and the tights will soon be hidden.

. . . .

A ball left in a pond before an overnight freeze will help to stop the pond from completely freezing over. If the ball is removed in the morning it leaves an air hole for fish and a water hole for other animals.

. . . .

Remove algae or blanket weed from a fish or garden pond by rotating a rough barked stick in it. To make it easier to remove the algae from the stick, cut a lengthways groove in it and the algae can be cut off with scissors. Use the algae as compost in the herb garden.

. . . .

After placing plants in a garden pool, wait three weeks for the water and plants to settle before introducing fish.

. . . .

To keep that green slime from collecting in the birdbath or
fountain, add a few copper pieces or coins.

. . . .

If potted plants are close to a pool, they should be moved away
when applying liquid fertilizer, as it could harm fish in the pond
and it also encourages algae growth.

# Hedges & Trees

*"A hedge between keeps friendship green."*
*—French Proverb*

A garden will benefit from having at least one length of hedge. It will give privacy and shelter from strong winds.

. . . .

In a small garden, hedges should be kept to the minimum. A fence covered with ivy, honeysuckle, or some other climbing plants may be preferable.

. . . .

Remember that tall evergreen hedges can block the sun and air to other plants in the garden.

. . . .

Hedging plants should be chosen on the basis that they will grow quickly, survive close planting, and be hardy and suitable for the soil in the area.

. . . .

Hedges can be grown from one species of plant or from several. All plants grown in a mixed hedge must be of similar habit.

. . . .

Flowering shrubs planted close together and minimally pruned can form a hedge, but will take up more space than a regular hedge.

. . . .

When planting a hedge, dig the strip of ground 3' (1 m) wide and two spits deep. Add a dressing of yard manure or compost to the bottom.

. . . .

Plant deciduous hedging in October or November, providing the weather is mild, damp, and calm. Do not plant in frosty or cold, dry weather. Planting can be done up until March.

. . . .

Evergreen hedging should be planted between mid-September and mid-October, but if this is not possible, then April or early May.

. . . .

All plants should be well furnished with shoots from the base. Bare, leggy plants are difficult to make bushy.

. . . .

Any long taproots should be shortened and the tops of evergreens can be cut back. Generally, plants should be 18" (50 cm) high and planted 18" (50 cm) apart in the row. Some varieties may need less or more spacing, so check with the garden center when buying the plants.

. . . .

If a dense hedge is required, two rows 18" (50 cm) apart can be planted, alternating the plants so that they are not opposite each other.

. . . .

Plants should be put in a little deeper than the soil line and the soil well firmed in around them.

· · · ·

Spring-planted hedging may need to be watered. Put mulch around them when the soil has warmed up to help conserve moisture. Spray lightly in the evenings of hot days.

· · · ·

In the early stages of growth, shoots arising from the base should be stopped when they are 9"–10" (22–25 cm) long. This ensures that a series of lateral shoots are sent out up the whole height of the hedge and encourages a thick base.

· · · ·

Most hedges should be trimmed twice a year, in early summer and in late summer or early autumn. This leaves it neat and tidy over the winter for growth to start again in the spring.

· · · ·

Keep the hedge at a height that is easy to reach without having to use steps or trestles. A hedge between 5–6' (1.5–2 m) is ideal.

· · · ·

To keep a base of a hedge leafy, cut into a pyramid shape in spring, so that the top is narrower than the base. If a hedge is pruned wider at the top than the bottom, the lower part will be shaded and the foliage will fall off, allowing the top growth to spread, compounding the problem. The narrow top also makes it easier to trim.

· · · ·

*"It used to be thought that our love of plants was an impractical but pure passion. But now, in the age of environmental crisis, we're discovering that gardening is essential to human life."*
—Jacqueline Heriteau

When using a ladder to cut a high hedge, it will be necessary to prevent it from sinking into the foliage. Get a piece of timber approximately 4' (1.3 m) in length and nail two short lengths of drainpipe the same width as your ladder, at right angles (making an "H" shape). Place the top edge of your ladder into the drainpipes. The plank spreads the weight across the hedge.

. . . .

There is a growth retardant that can be purchased and sprayed on the hedge after cutting to slow down the growth for the rest of the season.

. . . .

If a hedge is too dense, cut it back to the main stems on one side only. Let the hedge recover and produce new growth for a year, then cut back the other side.

. . . .

If a hedge is too tall, cut back every second shrub to within a few inches of the ground. New shoots should sprout around the severed trunks. Cut back the remaining shrubs the following year.

. . . .

Tree wounds over 1" (2.5 cm) in diameter can be dressed with a tree wound dressing available from most garden centers.

. . . .

To stop this protective dressing from cracking with sun exposure, it is important to make sure the wound is dry before applying the dressing to ensure good bonding.

. . . .

Check the coating several times during the first year and re-treat if cracked.

. . . .

As well as clipping, hedges should be kept free of pests, diseases, and weeds.

. . . .

Leave a space of 1'-2' (30–60 cm) between hedges and the foliage of other plants.

# HOW TO PLANT A TREE

A tree's dormant period—from late autumn after leaf drop to early spring before bud break—is the best time for planting.

. . . .

Prepare for planting by calling the local utility companies to locate your underground lines. Whatever form of tree you plant, the instructions are similar. The following method refers to balled-and-burlapped and container-grown trees. 1.) Measure the diameter of the tree's root ball with the shovel handle. Remove sod that's twice as wide as the root ball. Set the tree aside (pick it up by the root ball, not by the trunk). 2.) Dig a planting hole. Make sure it is deep enough so that the top of the root ball will align with ground level. Loosen soil in the bottom of the hole and around the sides. Peel the burlap back from the trunk but leave it on the root ball; it will decompose eventually. Remove any containers, plastic, twine, or wire encasements. Center tree in the hole. 3.) Refill the hole with soil. Do not fertilize. Crumble dirt clods, then settle the soil and eliminate air pockets around roots by watering the hole as you fill it. After the hole is completely backfilled and watered, apply mulch. Water again in a week, then again every week (unless 1" [2.5 cm] of rain falls) through the first growing season and prior to winter.

. . . .

When planting bare rooted trees and shrubs, spread the roots out like an umbrella; twisted roots stunt growth. As you cover the roots with soil, shake the plant from time to time to allow the soil to drop down well between them. Water well after planting.

. . . .

*"I think that if you shake the tree, you ought to be
around when the fruit falls to pick it up."*
*—Mary Cassatt*

Put support stakes in before you plant a new tree to avoid the
possibility of damaging the roots.

. . . .

To prevent snow damaging small conifers, when it is forecast,
tie the branches to the trunk with string or old nylon tights.
However, do not leave them tied for more than a day or two.

. . . .

When planting trees or other large plants, make sure they don't
adversely affect your neighbor's house or view.

## FRUIT TREES

Crab apple is the most commonly used ornamental fruit tree.
Cherry and plum trees make beautiful additions to the landscape;
they flower in early spring and then produce a crop of tasty fruit
in the summer.

. . . .

The best age to buy fruit trees such as apples, peaches, cherries,
plums, and pears for planting in the home garden is one to two
years old.

. . . .

Fruit trees can be planted at any time when they are dormant—
usually from November to the end of February.

. . . .

Do not plant fruit trees or shrubs near the vegetable garden.
Their needs are different—especially the specific spraying for
disease control.

. . . .

Dessert apples, gooseberries, and strawberries should be grouped
together as they require only a limited amount of nitrogen.
Cooking apples, plums, and bush and cane fruit need more, while
black currants will require a large amount.

. . . .

Raspberries and gooseberries like moderate shade, while other
fruits like full sunshine.

. . . .

Mulching fruit trees helps to conserve moisture, control weeds,
adds plant food as the mulch decays, and catches the fruit when it
drops, preventing bruising.

. . . .

Young, developing trees often set fruit that take the nourishment
needed to build up the tree framework. Most of these fruits
should be removed at an early stage.

. . . .

Sometimes older fruit trees set more fruit than they can hope to develop. Some thinning should be done, but not until the natural shedding has been completed, generally around mid-July.

. . . .

Branches of old fruit trees should be well propped to prevent them breaking when laden with fruit.

. . . .

Fruit trees are quite hardy, but the flowers are easily damaged by frost. To avoid this, cover the trees with a light piece of material or newspaper.

. . . .

If blossoms are only slightly frozen, cover to protect them from the early morning sun, as it is quick thawing that causes most damage.

. . . .

To evaluate pollination in apples, slice an apple crossways. There are five seed pockets with the potential of two seeds in each. If there are eight to ten fully developed seeds, then you should have a good crop. If there are less, then better pollination is required from more bees in the garden or a different variety of fruit tree.

. . . .

Soft fruit should be picked when it is cool and dry, early in the morning after the dew has lifted but before the sun warms the fruit. Plums should also be picked dry.

. . . .

If apples or pears are to be stored, then they are best picked dry—otherwise they should be spread out to dry after picking.

Check the ripeness of apples by gently lifting the fruit with the palm of the hand, while still attached to the tree. When ripe, the stalk will detach itself easily.

. . . .

If the garden is more than 600' (175 m) above sea level, it will be difficult to grow fruit trees satisfactorily, unless they have plenty of protection.

. . . .

To help keep fruit trees free from pests, allow chickens to feed under the trees to eat the insects and larvae.

. . . .

Store apples and pears separately, as apples should be left undisturbed while pears need to be checked regularly.

. . . .

Fig trees need their roots confined. Plant in a 3' (1 m) cubic hole, line the sides with concrete slabs, and fill with rubble.

## LEGENDS & LORE

In ancient Greece and Rome, the hawthorn was linked with hope, marriage, and babies. At wedding ceremonies, the bridal attendants wore its blossoms and the bride carried a bough. However, in medieval Europe, the hawthorn was regarded as an unlucky plant; bringing it into a house would cause the death of a member of the household. Anyone uprooting or cutting down a hawthorn bush in a "fairy fort" would have bad luck.

. . . .

The laurel is associated with fame and achievement. It was also believed by some that a person standing under a laurel tree would be shielded from infection by the plague, from lightning, and witches.

. . . .

The oak tree has a widespread association with thunder gods, probably due to the fact that oak seems to attract more lightning than other trees. To Northern European people, the oak leaf cluster was a token of heroism and victory. In literature, the oak denotes strength, masculinity, stability, and longevity.

. . . .

The olive tree provides oil but also food, fuel for lamps, medicine, an emollient for dry skin, and anointing oil for religious purposes. The olive is regarded as a symbol of peace, wealth, and a sign of safe travel.

. . . .

The weeping willow is a well-known symbol of unlucky love and mourning in the Western world. In the East, it has been associated with the springtime regeneration of nature, eternal friendship, patience, perseverance, and meekness. It is dangerous for cattle to eat willow leaves.

. . . .

The traditions with mistletoe are many. Kissing under the mistletoe is first found associated with the Greek festival of Saturnalia and later with primitive marriage rites. Mistletoe was believed to have the power of bestowing fertility. In Scandinavia, mistletoe was considered a plant of peace, under which enemies could declare a truce, or warring spouses could kiss and make up. In some parts of England, the Christmas mistletoe is burned on the twelfth night, lest all the boys and girls who have kissed under it never marry. And for those who wish to observe the correct etiquette: a man should pluck a berry when he kisses a woman under the mistletoe, and when the last berry is gone, there should be no more kissing!

# The Vegetable Patch

*"Hoeing: A manual method of severing roots from stems
of newly planted flowers and vegetables."*
—Henry Beard

## RAISED BEDS

Raised bed gardening has many benefits. It can save space, reduce water loss, and discourage weeds. Reducing foot traffic in the growing area reduces soil compaction. And concentrating organic matter in a defined area builds soil productivity.

• • • •

Creating raised beds takes a considerable amount of work at the beginning, so try one or two beds first. And then, if you are happy with the results, add more next season.

• • • •

To make simple raised beds, choose a well-drained site with adequate sunlight and a nearby water source. Beds should be only as wide as can be easily worked from either side, usually about 3' (1 m) and as long as required. If the soil is compacted, do not start to prepare the bed until the soil is dry enough to work. Spread a 2"-3" (5-7 cm) layer of organic material over the soil surface. Organic material can include compost, sawdust, ground bark, leaves, chipped pruning materials, or manure. Adding an additional source of nitrogen helps the organic material break down more efficiently. Rototill or dig in the organic material, nitrogen supplement, and soil down to a depth of at least 6" (15 cm). With a shovel and rake, shape the bed. Shovel a walkway area, about 18" (45 cm) wide, to a depth of 6" (15 cm). Add the excavated soil to the top of the bed. Finished raised beds should be at least 8"-12" (12–30 cm) higher than the paths. Level the top of the bed with a rake.

• • • •

Put sawdust, bark, or old carpet on the paths between beds for a less muddy walking surface.

. . . .

Raised beds don't have to be contained by wooden boards. Beds could be raised to waist-high level, if stooping is a problem.

. . . .

Remember that the higher the raised bed is, the quicker it will dry out, so monitor moisture carefully.

. . . .

Once the beds have been properly built, light digging or forking will then create a suitable bed for planting. As time goes on, soil will keep loosening and you will be able to garden almost year round.

## VEGETABLES

Instead of the hard work of getting up turf, and then having the problem of disposing of it, lay old paving slabs over the area to be made into a bed. Leave it for a month or more, then take the slabs up. All the grass will have died off. Dig the new patch and dig in some compost. It works best in the winter months when the ground is wet.

. . . .

Dig the vegetable garden during a dry spell in late autumn or early winter. The frost will make the soil crumbly and workable, ready to plant the seeds in the spring. Firm down the surface with your feet and level it off with a rake.

. . . .

Potatoes are the best crop to sow in a new vegetable garden. They help to clear the ground of weeds because during their cultivation they need plenty of hoeing and weed clearing. They also produce dense cover to inhibit weeds. Their extensive root system breaks up the soil. If the garden was previously grassland, the potatoes may suffer from wire-worm damage.

· · · ·

Make a careful decision on how many vegetables of each type to plant. A lot of water is lost through leaves, so in a dry year, large brassica can draw out valuable soil moisture.

· · · ·

If the garden is small, choose cut-and-come-again plants such as leaf lettuce and spinach, which will continue to crop from the same plant.

· · · ·

A three-course rotation plan should always be developed. Different groups of vegetables make different demands on the plant food in the soil, and they require different cultivation. The allotted garden should be divided into three and each plot cropped in turn—pod bulb and stem crops (peas, beans, leeks, celery), green crops (cabbage, broccoli, Brussels sprouts, kale) and root crops (carrots, turnips, potatoes, beetroot). Runner beans and onions are the only exceptions and can be grown in the same plot two or three years in succession.

• • • •

Seeds should be covered with soil two to four times their own smallest diameter. For early sowings, and in clay soils, cover a little less than the normal depth.

• • • •

When sowing carrot seeds, distribute a layer of ground coffee grinds. This not only helps the carrots to grow straight, but also helps to prevent carrot rust flies.

• • • •

Seedlings should be transplanted as soon as they form their first true leaves (these are the third and fourth leaves to form) and before they become crowded in the tray or pot.

• • • •

*"He who plants a garden, plants happiness."*
*—Chinese Proverb*

Rows of small vegetables should be thinned as soon as the individual plants begin to crowd each other and before there is the slightest chance of their becoming "leggy" for lack of light and air.

. . . .

To prevent peas being eaten by pests, fill a short length of plastic guttering with compost and sow peas along the length as normal. Hang guttering out of reach of pests. When seedlings are 2" (5 cm) tall, slide the compost and seedlings into a shallow trench in the garden.

. . . .

Runner bean and snap pea shoots should be supported with canes once the plants are around 6" (15 cm) tall. This will encourage them to climb.

. . . .

If cloches are not used to protect young pea or bean seedlings, then lightweight mesh netting must be placed over the row to protect from birds.

. . . .

Dig the roots of beans and peas into the ground in the autumn as they are high in nitrogen and beneficial to the next rotation crop.

. . . .

Always use two hands to pick peas to avoid pulling the plant out of the ground.

. . . .

Pinch out the tops of broad bean plants to encourage growth and plenty of flowers; this also discourages blackflies.

. . . .

Avoid planting carrots in very stony ground, in fresh manure, or in heavy clods, as these cause misshapen roots.

. . . .

Sow carrot seeds sparingly to minimize the need for thinning. Any disturbance of foliage attracts the carrot fly.

. . . .

After thinning carrot plants or hoeing around them, remove all traces of thinnings and water lightly with a watering can or hose to dampen down the aroma from the foliage.

. . . .

Carrots, beets, and turnips should be stored in a cool, dark place, packed in sand or slightly moist peat moss, or in boxes covered with bags containing sand, leaves, or peat moss.

. . . .

When planting cucumber, pumpkins, or marrow, place a plastic collar around the seed (use an old bottomless pot or the center of a large plastic mineral bottle). When watering the plant, do not water inside the "collar" and this will keep the area dry around the plant and avoid "collar rot." Another method is to submerge a pot next to each plant; when they need watering, pour water directly down below soil level.

. . . .

Do not plant string beans, corn, cucumbers, squash, pumpkins, or spinach seeds until the soil is well warmed.

. . . .

Avoid watering cucumbers with cold or chlorinated water; keep a container of water in your greenhouse.

. . . .

Plant cauliflower seeds in individual pots and transplant carefully without disturbing the roots. Space the plants 4" (10 cm) apart and 8" (20 cm) between rows. Never allow the plants to dry out.

. . . .

Brassica plants benefit from being planted deep in order to establish a strong root system to support their large heads. Plant with the soil up to the level of their basal leaves.

. . . .

To intercrop vegetables, plant rows of quick-growing crops, such as lettuce, radishes, or spinach between widely spaced, slower growing items, such as celery, peas, and tomatoes. If carefully planned, intercropping can result in producing more food from a given area. This can also be done with trees and shrubs and berry bushes, and herbs can be planted between fruit trees.

. . . .

In a small garden, it is best to plant early potatoes. Each year use fresh certified seed tubers, as saved potato tubers can have virus contamination. For better results, choose seed tubers about the size of a hen egg rather than cutting up large ones. Early potato tubers should have two sprouts (rub out any excess). Main crop tubers should have numerous sprouts.

. . . .

Make sure that potatoes are always well earthed up as this stops them getting frosted or being exposed to the sun and becoming green and poisonous.

. . . .

Harvest spinach frequently as it is prone to bolting, especially in light soils and dry conditions.

. . . .

To improve the growth of leeks, add a little soot to the soil.

• • • •

When planting leek plants, trim the root and leaf tips. Drop the plant into a 6"- (15 cm) deep hole and fill the hole with water.

• • • •

Weeding between onion rows should be done by hand, as hoeing will damage the shallow roots.

• • • •

Small onion sets will produce onions that are less likely to bolt.

• • • •

Plant onion sets, shallots, or garlic with a trowel—do not push the bulbs into the soil. With shallots and garlic, leave the shoot showing through on the surface.

• • • •

Plant garlic cloves in January: poke 4" (10 cm) holes in the ground with the end of a rake and drop the garlic cloves into them.

• • • •

Squashes, pumpkins, and onions require dry storage. The squashes and pumpkins should be "cured" for a week or two and then stored on a shelf in a cool, dark room. Onions should be kept in the dark, in a dry place.

• • • •

Save some seeds from small red peppers and plant two or three seeds at a time in yogurt pots. When they are a couple of inches high, repot in a medium-sized plant pot. You will soon have an attractive indoor plant, and a supply of chilies.

. . . .

Pick Brussels sprouts from the bottom of the stem, as the more mature sprouts are below the younger ones. Cut off the sprouts rather than pulling them to avoid damaging the stems.

. . . .

Watercress can be grown in an area of fairly damp soil. Overwatering will diminish the flavor.

. . . .

When feeding tomatoes with liquid, it's easy to scorch the leaves. To avoid this happening, pour from the watering can using a piece of 1¼" (3 cm) drainpipe as a funnel directing the feed straight to the base of the plant, away from the leaves.

. . . .

Pinching out the side-shoots on tomato plants is a good way to propagate them. If the side-shoots are pulled off the plant when they are about 4" (10 cm) long and planted in moist soil, they will usually root and produce extra plants for free.

. . . .

Outdoor tomato plants should be of the bush variety as they are less labor intensive and do not require tying in or side-shooting.

. . . .

*"In order to live off a garden, you practically have to live in it."*
*—Frank McKinney*

Shake 1 teaspoon Epsom salt around tomato plants or peppers to green up the foliage.

. . . .

When thinning larger plants, use a knife to cut the stem at ground level. This thins the plant population effectively and does not damage root systems of the remaining vegetables, as pulling out unnecessary plants will do.

. . . .

Don't waste vegetable thinnings. Small onions may be used as scallions or spring onions. Baby carrots can be added whole to soups and stir-fries. Salad greens, mustards, cabbage, and broccoli thinnings can be used in a mixed salad. Or the thinnings of many kinds of vegetables can be used for transplanting, if additional plants are wanted.

. . . .

A thin coat of newly mown grass cuttings spread around their bases will help control caterpillars on brassica (cabbage, broccoli, etc).

. . . .

When hoeing the ground, only disturb the top ½" (1.25 cm) of soil. Going deeper than this will cause more weed seeds to germinate.

# The Herb Garden

*"When young 'sow wild oats'; but when old, grow sage."*
*—H. J. Byron*

## LEGENDS & LORE

Chicory was believed to have the power of making its possessor invisible. It could also open doors or boxes if it was held against the locks. These charms, however, would only work if the plant was gathered at noon or at midnight on St James's Day (July 25th). It had to be cut with gold and in silence; if the gatherer spoke during the operation, he would die, either at once or shortly afterward.

· · · ·

Parsley should never be transplanted, but grown from seed. It takes seven weeks to germinate and one belief is that it grows down to the devil and then up again. When the parsley does grow, it should be picked, not cut; and never give it away, as misfortune is sure to follow. Parsley is not only a sure sign of a strong woman, but it will only grow outside the home of an honest man.

· · · ·

Basil stands for "animosity," and the planting method shows why. A gardener should curse with great gusto while planting basil seeds; otherwise they won't grow! It is also reputed to stimulate sensuality. In New Mexico, carrying basil in your pockets is supposed to attract money to them.

· · · ·

Aphrodite first cultivated marjoram, so ancient Greeks wore wreaths of sweet marjoram as wedding flowers. They also considered it an antidote for snakebite, and if this failed, they planted it on the grave to help the dead sleep in peace.

. . . .

Rosemary has been associated with memory, so students studying for examinations used to wear garlands of rosemary on their heads. It is also linked with fidelity and love, so it was used in wedding garlands. A rosemary plant flourishing outside a house is a sign that the wife is the boss of the household.

. . . .

Sage thrives in the garden of a woman who rules her household, and her husband, firmly. Another belief is that the sage plant reflects the fortune of the man of the house, flourishing when he's prospering and withering when he isn't.

## HERBS

Herbs can be grown in a separate part of the garden—preferably near the kitchen—or they can be grown in pots or containers or with other flowering plants. They like a sunny place and light, fertile, well-drained soil, but they are generally hardy enough to be grown in most soil. Herbs are short-term plants—some are annuals and must be planted each season from seed. The perennials will need to be renewed every two to three years.

. . . .

*BASIL,* also called sweet basil, is a pleasant-smelling annual plant with a spicy taste. The leaves are light-green, tender, and smooth. Basil grows well in the garden or as a potted plant. Cooks favor it for all kinds of tomato dishes. It can also be added to soups, vegetables, and Italian dishes. Start basil in pots indoors or outdoors if the soil temperature is above 50°F/10°C. Cover seeds with fine soil, to a depth of only ⅛" (3 mm). Gently press down the soil over seeds and water with a fine spray. Seeds should germinate in one to two weeks. Keep the soil moist. Shade young basil plants if the weather is sunny, as they wither easily. Thin seedlings by cutting unwanted plants off at the soil surface with scissors. Basil plants should eventually be planted 12"–18" (28–45 cm) apart. After seedlings are 6" (15 cm) high, pinch off the tops for bushier plants. Harvest basil leaves regularly. Water and fertilize the plants frequently. Pinch off the flowers to keep the plant from going to seed.

· · · ·

*BAY* is a large herb plant that grows into a small tree or tall evergreen bush. Its aromatic leaves are used to garnish pâté, in fish dishes, or in a bouquet garni to flavor soups and casseroles.

· · · ·

*"There are no gardening mistakes, only experiments."*
*—Janet Kilburn Phillips*

CHERVIL is a white flowered, hardy annual raised from seed. Its foliage is similar to parsley and it likes a shady area. It has a delicate, slightly spicy fragrance and can be used in soups, sauces, savory butter, and potato salad.

. . . .

CHIVES are small perennial, onion-like plants that grow in a clumping fashion. In early spring the leaves are topped with purple flowers. Plants can be purchased or grown from seed. Established clumps can be divided and transplanted. Garlic chives are similar in appearance to regular chives but have a slightly garlicky flavor. Use chives fresh, cut off from the plant as required, to give a mild onion flavor.

. . . .

DILL is an annual herb whose leaves and seeds are popular flavorings for pickles, cucumber, and fish dishes. It is a tall plant with small yellow, umbrella-shaped flower heads and feathery foliage, similar to fennel. Dill seeds can be planted in the autumn or early spring.

. . . .

FENNEL is similar to dill but is perennial and hardier. However, the plants can become very large, so it is best to grow annually. It will self-seed freely. The leaves and bulb have an aniseed flavor. Use the leaves with fish and the seeds with eggs, cheese, vegetables, and in cakes.

. . . .

*LEMON BALM* is a lemon-scented plant used in iced drinks and hot teas. It spreads rapidly so it should be planted in a container in the ground or frequently cut. Growing to a height of nearly 2' (60 cm), its oval leaves have slightly serrated edges and clusters of small white flowers. Start from seed or small plants. It will self-seed or can be propagated by root division.

. . . .

*MINTS* such as peppermint and spearmint are hardy perennials used to make herbal tea, flavor drinks and liqueurs, and to make mint sauce. Mints are the easiest to grow perennial herbs. They grow profusely in sun or shade. Plant in moist soil in sunken pots in the garden to stop spreading. Use the leaves and flowering tops both fresh and dried.

. . . .

*OREGANO/MARJORAM* can be grown from seed sown in the spring or propagated by cuttings. They are low-growing, clump-forming, slightly woody perennials. Shoot cuttings can be taken in late summer and the plant should be replaced every two to three years. Cut the tender tops of both herbs just as flowers begin. Add oregano to Italian-type sauces, pizza, and meats. Marjoram can be used in stuffing or for flavoring meats, and it enhances mushroom soup.

. . . .

*PARSLEY* is a very popular mild-flavored herb. It is a densely leafy biennial, but is best grown annually from seed. There are curly and flat-leafed varieties. The curly is popular for its appearance, but the flat leafed had a stronger flavor. It can be slow to germinate, but watering with hot water after planting the seeds can speed up the process. Once the leaves appear, it grows rapidly. It's regularly used as a garnish and for flavoring a wide variety of meat and vegetable dishes.

. . . .

*ROSEMARY* is an evergreen bush with leaves like long, oval pine needles. It should be trimmed frequently or renewed every few years or it will become straggly. Since it is a tender plant, it should be brought indoors during the winter. The plant can be started from seed or propagated from a cutting. Purchased plants should be about 12" (28 cm) tall. It is highly aromatic and used to give added flavor to lamb, poultry, and roasted vegetables.

. . . .

*SAGE* is a woody perennial growing to about 2' (60 cm) in height. It has gray-green soft, furry leaves and blue flowers. Cut the plant back after the flowers are gone. It can be started from seed or propagated from cutting, layering, or root division.

. . . .

*TARRAGON* has delicate upright shoots with soft, narrow, willow-like leaves. It is excellent for flavoring salad dressing, chicken, and fish. It is best starting with a plant, but can be propagated by cuttings or root division. Should be brought indoors during the winter or else well covered outdoors.

. . . .

*"When planning for a year, plant corn.*
*When planning for a decade, plant trees.*
*When planning for life, train and educate people."*
—Chinese Proverb

*THYME* is a shrubby perennial herb. It is a small plant with very tiny gray-green leaves. Purplish flowers are formed on the ends of the stems. New plants can be started from seed (indoors), cuttings, or root division. For best growth, thyme should be replanted every three to four years. To use, remove the top one-third portion of the plant when in full bloom and spread on newspaper to dry. Then strip the leaves and flowering tops from the stem and store in tightly closed containers. Use in stuffings and meat dishes.

## METHODS OF DRYING HERBS

Tender-leafed herbs such as basil, lemon balm, tarragon, and mint have a high moisture content and must be dried rapidly in a dark place to keep their deep-green leaf shade.

• • • •

Woodier herbs such as sage, rosemary, and thyme can be partially dried in the sun.

## DRYING HERBS

Rinse herbs in clean water and tie in bunches with string or elastic bands.

. . . .

Hang upside down outside in the sunshine, in an airing cupboard, in the kitchen, or in an oven at a low temperature.

## BAG DRYING

To prepare plants for drying, remove blossoms from the herb plant and rinse the leaves on the stem in cold water to remove soil.

. . . .

Allow plants to drain on absorbent towels until dry. Then place the herbs in a paper bag and tie the stems. Leave 1"–2" (2.5–5 cm) of the stems exposed. This allows the plant oil to flow from the stems to the leaves.

. . . .

Place the bag in a warm, dry location. In about one to two weeks, when the leaves become brittle, tap them free of the stems and the leaves will fall into the bag. Store leaves in an airtight container away from the light.

## TRAY DRYING

Clean herbs as for bag drying, but the heavy stalks can be discarded.

. . . .

Put the leafed stems one layer deep on a tray in a dark, ventilated room.

· · · ·

Turn over the herbs occasionally for uniform drying.

· · · ·

The leaves are ready for storage when they are dry and the stems are tough.

## MICROWAVE DRYING

Use a microwave oven to dry herbs.

· · · ·

Place the herbs between paper towels and set them on the rack.

· · · ·

Close the door and turn the microwave on for about two to three minutes. Then check for dryness; the leaves should feel brittle and should crumble easily. If they are not done, leave them in the oven for thirty seconds longer. Although this process actually cooks the herbs, the end product is the same as air-drying. Store the dried herbs in closed containers.

*"It takes both rain and sunshine to make a rainbow."*—Unknown

## STORING HERBS

When the herbs are dry, either keep the leaves whole or crumble and pack into small jars.

. . . .

Cover and label with the date, then store in a cool, dark place.

. . . .

The shelf life of many herbs is one to two years, but this period is shorter if herbs are exposed to light, heat, and open air.

. . . .

When herb seeds are to be used for cooking, the seeds should be stored whole and ground up as needed.

## FREEZING

Herbs may also be frozen.

. . . .

Rinse herbs in cold water and blanch in boiling, unsalted water for fifty seconds. Cool quickly in ice water, package, and freeze.

. . . .

Dill, parsley, chives, and basil can be frozen without blanching.

## GARDEN HINTS

Bats are useful in a garden as they eat approximately half their weight in insects each night. Bats are also very instrumental in plant pollination.

. . . .

Plant nasturtiums, dill, lavender, thyme, hyssop, or sage around the base of apple trees or other plants to control aphids.

. . . .

If you are having problems getting your runner beans to set, either try spraying them with sugar water or planting sweet peas in the same row. Both methods will attract pollinators.

. . . .

To store and ripen green tomatoes, harvest tomatoes free of blemishes, then wash and dry them. Place in a box with four ripe apples. Keep in a cool place around 50–60°F/10–15°C. The ethylene gas produced will help ripen the fruit.

. . . .

Don't throw out that old carpet; turn it upside down on a newly dug patch of soil or between vegetable beds to use it as an inexpensive weed blanket. Slit through when planting and then cover entirely with bark or gravel.

. . . .

Ladybugs are a great gardener's friend. Always put them on plants suffering from aphids as they just love to eat them. To attract ladybugs to your garden, plant Jerusalem artichokes.

. . . .

Although we may not like spiders, they do eat a lot of insects, and without them the garden would soon be overrun with pests.

• • • •

Encourage the birds to come into your garden, particularly with a birdbath. Birds eat a lot of garden pests and they are lovely to watch.

• • • •

When filling plant pots with compost, only fill to within 1" (2–3 cm) of the rim to allow room for watering.

• • • •

When you've boiled eggs, use the leftover water to pour between the cracks in the sidewalk or stone path to prevent weeds growing.

# Working in the Garden

*"It will never rain roses. When we want to have more roses, we must plant more roses."*
—George Eliot

## FERTILIZERS

An array of fertilizers can now be purchased and they are all blended for every possible type of plant and every possible circumstance.

. . . .

There are three main ingredients contained in varying amounts in all fertilizers and these are nitrogen (N), phosphate (P), and potash (K).

. . . .

Nitrogen encourages leafy growth. Phosphate encourages roots to form and is valuable at planting time. Potash stimulates flowering and fruiting.

. . . .

Fertilizer should always be spread as uniformly as possible in the area where it is required. Labels on the container should specify the dosing instructions.

. . . .

Always wear gloves and wash hands after handling fertilizer.

. . . .

Fertilizer for organic gardens: fill a container one-quarter full of barnyard manure or well-rotted compost (never use dog or cat feces). Fill to half full with water. Over the next 24 to 48 hours, stir several times during the day. After 48 hours, your fertilizer is ready to use. Dilute the liquid to a light amber color with water. Pour 1 pt (500 ml) of diluted solution around each plant when setting out, or later as necessary to force growth.

. . . .

When removing nettles from the garden, put them in a bucket and cover with water. Leave for two to three weeks and the resulting strongly smelling liquid makes an excellent fertilizer, especially good for tomatoes.

. . . .

Place old banana skins around the base of rose plants as fertilizer.

. . . .

Dissolve 1 lb (450 g) dried milk in a little hot water, add to 1 gal (5 ltr) cold water. Spray on tomatoes, lettuce, and cucumbers when planting and every ten days afterward.

## PRUNING

Early spring and late winter is the best time to prune many shrubs and small trees.

. . . .

Shrubs that bloom in summer and autumn generally develop flowers on the current seasons' growth and should be pruned before the first flush of growth in the spring.

. . . .

Shrubs that bloom in the spring or winter should be pruned immediately after flowering has finished.

. . . . .

In early summer, prune evergreens that are not in flower. Prune conifers in late summer or early autumn. Prune other evergreens after flowering.

. . . . .

Pruning is practiced to maintain plant health, control plant growth, and encourage flowering and fruiting. These objectives should be remembered as you prune.

. . . . .

Pruning should encourage plant health, not plant disease, so it is important to prune properly using the correct pruning tools.

. . . . .

For twigs and light branches, hand pruning shears or secateurs can be used.

. . . . .

Loppers may be used for branches up to 1½" (4 cm) thick. Use a pruning saw for larger branches.

. . . . .

*"Gardening requires lots of water—most of it in
the form of perspiration."*
*—Lou Erickson*

Hedge shears or clippers should be used to trim closely clipped
hedges only.

. . . .

All tools should be kept sharp. Sharp tools cut easier and avoid
bruising the plant tissue. Bruising the plant causes slower healing
of the wound and causes an increase in the probability of disease.

. . . .

A clean cut should be made; the cut surface should have a
smooth surface, not a rough one that looks as if the tissue has
been torn or pulled.

. . . .

Care should be taken not to damage the plant around the cut, or
rip or tear the bark above or below the cut. The cambium layer,
a thin layer of cells just below the bark, is important in wound
healing and it is easily damaged.

. . . .

Do not twist or turn the shears as you cut because you will
damage the plant as well as the shears.

. . . .

Unless a shrub is a topiary or part of a formal hedge, it should not
be closely clipped but allowed to develop naturally and pruned to
keep in shape.

. . . .

First remove all dead, diseased, or injured branches. If necessary, thin out the plant. Remove branches that cross each other or they will become entangled. If the shrub still looks too thick, remove some of the older branches. Remove any branches that are distinctly different from the rest of the shrub. Cut back any very long growth to a bud.

. . . .

To reduce the size of a shrub, cut back each branch 4"–6" (10–15 cm), to a new bud. Do not use hedge shears; cut each branch separately.

. . . .

Prune hybrid tea and floribunda roses in March. Cut out dead, diseased, or thin wood and trim back the main shoots. When cutting back main shoots, count buds from the base of each shoot and cut just above the second or third one. The length of the shoot is less important than the number of buds.

. . . .

Shrub roses are best pruned in winter. As both old and modern roses produce most of their flowers on shoots produced from old wood, prune lightly. Remove dead, thin, and decayed wood and shorted main stems by one third.

. . . .

Prune rambling roses in the autumn. Cut untidy, flowered shoots right down to the base and tie new shoots to the trellis or support. If there are a few new shoots, leave some of the flowered shoots in place, cutting back just a little.

. . . .

*"To a gardener there is nothing more exasperating
than a hose that just isn't long enough."*
*—Cecil Roberts*

Climbing roses are also best pruned in the autumn. Remove any crossing or thin shoots and reduce the height of the main stems by about one third. This prevents them being blown about by the wind. Remove any side shoots that spoil the shape and cut back the others by about two thirds.

. . . .

Miniature roses should be pruned in March. Cut off any dead, diseased, or thin wood and trim back the main stems.

## WATERING

For successful gardening, it is important to know when and how to water.

. . . .

There are no specific rules to follow, because when to water and how much to water depends on the kinds of plants, type of soil, time of year, and the weather conditions.

. . . .

Water only when plants need watering. The leaves of many plants will begin to curl in the early stages of a water shortage. Later, the leaves will become very limp and the plant is said to have "wilted." Plants should be watered before they wilt. Allowing them to wilt frequently will result in excessive leaf drop. Also, if plants are allowed to remain wilted for several days, they may never revive.

. . . .

Some plants may not show symptoms of a water shortage until it is too late. These plants should be watered when the soil around them feels dry and crumbly.

• • • •

New plantings will need special attention, as when they were in containers in the nursery, water was applied daily.

• • • •

During the first couple of seasons after being planted, new plants still have small root systems and can only absorb water from a limited soil area.

• • • •

Check lawn grass for wilting—if the edges of the grass leaves start to curl and take on a dull bluish-gray color, water the lawn immediately.

• • • •

Lawns should be watered in the early morning, when winds and temperatures are low. Late morning, midday, and afternoon irrigation usually results in loss of water from evaporation.

• • • •

When watering, give the soil a thorough soaking. Frequent, light sprinklings waste water and do not satisfy the water requirements of a plant growing in a hot, dry soil. It can also promote shallow root systems, and these increase susceptibility to damage during dry spells.

. . . .

Water should be applied only as fast as the soil will absorb it. Watering with a hose nozzle turned on full force can do more damage than good. Fast-flowing water runs off quickly, carrying soil with it and exposing plant roots to the sun. Sprinkler systems are more efficient.

. . . .

Another method of watering is drip or trickle irrigation. Drip irrigation supplies plants with constant moisture at a low delivery rate through the use of low-pressure plastic tubing installed on or below the ground surface.

. . . .

Low-pressure nozzles attached to plastic tubing release water at a slow rate into the soil around a plant. By wetting only the root area of the plant, there is a big saving in water, weeds are not encouraged to grow, and plant growth is accelerated. This increased growth occurs because the plant is not subjected to wet and dry cycles that normally occur with other irrigation methods.

. . . .

Garden plants should be watered most when they are maturing— flowers as the buds open, potatoes in flower, lettuces as they form a head, etc.

. . . .

*"Irrigation of the land with seawater desalinated
by fusion power is ancient. It's called 'rain'."*
*—Michael McClary*

Put a timer switch on sprinklers so they go on and off
automatically and don't waste water.

## WATER-WISE TIPS IN A DROUGHT

Know your soil. Does it retain moisture or does it dry out quickly?
Is the soil heavy in clay or rocks and gravel?

. . . .

Plant the right plants for the right soils. If an area is often wet,
plant thirsty plants there.

. . . .

Use native plants in your landscape—they require less care and
water than ornamental varieties.

. . . .

Place plants in groups according to the amount of water they need.

. . . .

If you have a slope, place lower-water-demand plants at higher
elevations and those that need more water at lower elevations.
The water from the higher areas will trickle down to the plants
that demand more moisture.

. . . .

Prioritize watering—take care of new and young plantings, then
more mature trees and shrubs.

. . . .

Water in the early morning to take advantage of the cooler temperatures and reduce evaporation.

. . . .

Water slowly, deeply, and infrequently to avoid water runoff.

. . . .

Make sure the hose or sprinkler does not leak, and avoid placing watering devices where they waste water.

. . . .

Help garden soils by using mulches, which dramatically reduce water evaporation from soils. Increase the mulch layers to 3"-4" (7.5-10 cm) thick.

. . . .

When mulching, ensure trees, shrubs, and plants have a basin of mulch around them. During a drought the water tends to run off quickly and not soak down into the soil. Creating a basin around plants holds the water in until it has an opportunity to soak into the ground.

. . . .

Don't fertilize or prune. Plants should not be encouraged to grow, and both pruning and fertilizing can encourage new growth. Fertilizers are salts, and without much water, the salts can build to harmful levels.

. . . .

Remove any dead or weakened plant tissues to avoid secondary problems.

. . . .

Control weeds. They compete with useful plants for water.

. . . .

Shelter container plants by moving them to shady areas. This will reduce water loss due to evaporation.

. . . .

Use a drip watering system. This can save up to 60 percent of the water used by sprinkler systems.

. . . .

Raise your lawn mower cutting height; longer grass blades help shade each other, cut down on evaporation, and inhibit weed growth.

. . . .

Consider letting the lawn go dormant; most lawn grasses will rebound when rains return.

. . . .

Consider reducing your lawn and grassy areas in favor of more creative gardens, such as those that use more stone and drought-resistant perennial plants that have deeper root systems.

. . . .

As a general rule, plants with gray or silvery foliage are the most drought-tolerant. They have fine hairs on their leaves that shade the leaf surface. Also consider using succulent plants (yucca, etc.).

. . . .

*"Compost—because a rind is a terrible thing to waste."*
*—Unknown*

Use recycled water whenever you can. "Recycled water" includes rainwater collected from rooftops, cooking water, or any other water that has not been used for humans or animals.

## COMPOST

Compost is organic matter that has broken down. Grass clippings, potato peelings, onion tops, and other vegetative waste material can be made into a valuable soil conditioner and used as plant food for garden beds in the autumn by remaining in a compost heap during the summer.

• • • •

Compost can be used in several ways. It provides a good usable soil amendment for the garden and is less expensive than peat. Incorporated into the soil or around plants, it is beneficial in improving soil texture, water-holding capacity, and nutrient retention. Compost can be used on the soil surface as mulch to control weeds and conserve moisture. Or mix compost with sterilized soil and use it for potting plants.

• • • •

Other materials such as leaves, waste from fresh summer vegetables, shredded paper, or sawdust can be layered in to make excellent compost.

• • • •

Old weeds can be added, but we only use weeds that haven't flowered, otherwise you could add weed seed to the compost.

• • • •

Do not add dog or cat manure, as their worming treatment can also kill off composting worms.

• • • •

Avoid adding meat and bones as they attract flies, rats, and other vermin.

• • • •

Do not include citrus peels, as they are too acidic for worms.

• • • •

Choose an out-of-the-way location for the compost area, since the heap may appear untidy. Choose a location that is convenient to the gardening area and to the kitchen door.

• • • •

Decomposition of the plant matter will require heat and moisture for quick breakdown. The summer sun will provide the heat, but the heap must be soaked occasionally to give it moisture.

• • • •

Animal manure is a rich, valuable garden soil additive and may be used between the layers of compost. The heat generated by the manure will induce quick decomposition of raw compost.

• • • •

The compost should be turned with a garden fork from time to time to aerate and to promote even decomposition.

• • • •

Cover the heap to keep excess rain from leaching out nutrients, keep stray wildlife away, and to "heat up" the pile.

· · · ·

Save old tea bags and put one or two in the bottom of plant pots to help retain moisture. Also use tea bags in the bottom of runner bean trenches.

· · · ·

Paper from an office shredder will rot well in a compost heap.

· · · ·

Make a 3 ft (1 m) cube with four posts and chicken wire as a leaf mold cage. Leaves rot more slowly than garden debris, so it's best to rot them separately. Press the leaves down firmly to compress them. It takes about eighteen months to have a rich mulch.

· · · ·

Always cover old potato tubers with other debris when they are put in the compost. This prevents any with blight fungus from sprouting and spreading spores that could infect a new season's crop.

· · · ·

Do not reuse old seedling compost, as disease organisms may be present and the nutrients have been mostly used up.

. . . .

Coffee grounds make an excellent mulch for plants that require acidic soil like blueberries, rhododendrons, and roses.

. . . .

Banana skins placed around rose bushes will rot down and provide nutrients.

. . . .

Getting water into peat-based potting mixes isn't easy. For small amounts, put the mix into a plastic bag, add water, and then knead the bag. For larger amounts, use a container such as a wheelbarrow, add the mix, then scoop out a center hole and add warm (not cold) water, continually blending. Never add the mix to water; instead, always add water to the mix.

. . . .

A light sprinkling of fertilizer between layers of added compost will aid in decomposition and replace the nitrogen used in breaking down raw materials into compost.

## MULCHING

A layer of organic material several inches thick buffers the soil against compaction from the harsh effects of heavy rain and baking sun, and helps the soil retain oxygen so it can support vigorous plant roots. It improves any soil by blending valuable organic material, or humus, into its top layer as the mulch gradually decomposes.

. . . .

A mulch helps conserve water by absorbing rainfall and preventing runoff. Soil covered by a layer of organic mulch stays damp much longer between rains or watering because the mulch blocks evaporation.

. . . .

A good layer of organic mulch between newly planted ground cover plants discourages weeds during the time the plants need to grow larger, knit together, and cover the soil on their own.

. . . .

Trees and shrubs thrive on mulch, too. Circles of organic material under them not only condition the soil and improve its fertility, but they also create a barrier to prevent injury to their trunks and stems from lawn mowers and string trimmers.

. . . .

A layer of organic mulch on the bare soil in a garden shelters many kinds of beneficial organisms. Ground spiders and ants nest in rich organic material along the edges of lawns. These insects prey on pest insect larvae and eggs in the soil under the lawn and garden beds.

. . . .

Avoid spreading mulch too thickly. A layer over 2"–3" (5 cm–7 cm) can become a suffocating blanket blocking air and moisture from the soil. This causes plant roots to gravitate toward the soil surface in search of these essentials. In cases where surface tree roots are a problem, mulch lightly to improve the appearance of the yard, but don't try to bury the roots.

. . . .

Organic mulch inevitably breaks down over time, and the mulch layer becomes thinner. Add mulch periodically, usually in the autumn.

. . . .

Shredded paper is a suitable mulch for protecting soil and discouraging weeds. If it becomes unsightly when rains wet it down, cover it with a thin layer of leaves or bark nuggets.

. . . .

During the winter, fluctuating temperatures alternately freeze and thaw the soil. This often disturbs plant roots and may leave bulbs or plants out of the soil. A winter mulch will not prevent soil from freezing, but it gives insulation to maintain more even low temperatures.

. . . .

Add a mound of mulch to roses to prepare them for winter.

## TYPES OF MULCH

Fallen leaves are a good mulch for bare soil in a garden.

. . . .

Shred or chop leaves to stop them matting,
which will block water from the soil.

. . . .

Gravel is an appropriate mulch for arid landscapes and beds with plants that need good drainage, such as rock gardens.

. . . .

Pine needles give a brown covering for the soil. Use them around acid-loving plants such as conifers, rhododendrons, and holly bushes.

. . . .

Wood chips are long-lasting and inexpensive. Allow them to age for a few weeks, then spread them on paths and under trees and woody plants.

. . . .

Leaf mold (partially decomposed leaves) contributes valuable organic matter to the soil as it decomposes. Use it for plants in woodland settings and informal gardens.

## HOW TO MULCH A TREE

When mulching an established tree with grass growing beneath it, put a layer of cardboard over the lawn before spreading the mulch. This will keep the grass from penetrating the mulch. Make the cardboard collar 2'-3' (60–90 cm) wide. Moisten to soften and easily conform to the contours of the ground and the root flare at the base of the trunk. Then cover it with wood chips.

# Getting Rid
# of Garden Pests

*"One of the worst mistakes you can make as a gardener*
*is to think you're in charge."*
—*Janet Gillespie*

# ANTS

Ants are attracted by sweet foods and are generally harmless
apart from the hills they make, but they can assist in the
spreading of aphids from plant to plant.

. . . .

Locate the ants' nest by sprinkling a little sugar and watch where
the ants carry it.

. . . .

If the nest cannot be found, identify where they are entering the
house and the run they are using—they seem to use the same thin
route. Place some proprietary ant powder or bait outside in this
run. Make sure it is out of reach of children and pets.

. . . .

Locate the ants' hill and sprinkle a liberal amount of talcum
powder around and on it. The ants dislike talc and will move their
colony several feet. Continue sprinkling the talc until the ants are
moved to where you want them.

. . . .

Boiling water poured into/onto the nest also works quite well.

. . . .

Put some water in an empty jam jar; make sure there is some jam on the edge of the jar and this may tempt some of them for a swim.

. . . .

Apparently ants never cross a chalk line, so get out the chalk and draw a line wherever ants tend to march.

. . . .

To deter ants, spray vinegar around doors, appliances, and along other areas where they are located.

. . . .

Dried cinnamon is a good ant deterrent and is very effective in places that chemicals cannot be used, e.g., around ponds.

. . . .

Ants hate peppermint. Mix some drops of oil with water in a sprayer and spray wherever there are ants. This is also really effective indoors.

. . . .

To get rid of ants, mix a small bottle of clove oil in a large watering can with a rose sprinkler. Sprinkle this over the area where the ants are. First the flying ants leave the nest in droves, then the soldier ants will follow them on foot.

*"How pleasant the lives of the birds must be,*
*living in love in a leafy tree."*
—Mary Howitt

## APHIDS

Greenfly and blackfly aphids attack a wide range of outdoor and greenhouse plants, trees, and shrubs.

. . . .

Their color varies from green, black, or reddish to almost white or bluish.

. . . .

The body is plump, semitransparent, winged, or wingless. They often exude a sticky honeydew on which a sooty mold grows.

. . . .

All are sucking insects and may carry diseases.

. . . .

They usually attack the underside of the leaves or the tips of shoots but they can also attack the roots of some plants.

. . . .

Early detection and action is essential. Leaf-curling, malformation, and discoloration occurs soon after an attack.

. . . .

A more-or-less-organic way of controlling aphids is to make a garlic tea by crushing and then boiling a few bulbs. Allow to cool and then spray. Add a few drops of washing-up liquid to the mixture brew to assist adhesion.

• • • •

Don't throw out old soap bars; melt them down in hot water and put them in a spray bottle to use in the greenhouse. The result is an effective aphid-killer.

• • • •

Proprietary sprays such as malathion, nicotine, derris, or pyrethrum can be used, making sure that the insects are covered. Systemic insecticides can also be used.

• • • •

On fruit trees, use a winter egg-killing spray.

• • • •

Root infestations are best dealt with by pulling up the root stumps as soon as possible and burning them.

• • • •

To get rid of greenflies on roses, in the spring, crush a clove of garlic and bury it at the roots of the rosebush.

• • • •

A simple way of removing greenflies and larvae from plants is to use strips of sticky tape. If placed lightly on a leaf or stem, it lifts the pests off without the tape sticking to the plant.

## BIRDS AND BEES

Hang old CDs around the garden to deter birds from attacking fruit during the daytime.

• • • •

Bees are not harmful unless provoked, trapped, or you are unfortunately in their line of flight.

• • • •

If there is a swarm of bees in your garden, do not attempt to remove it yourself. Contact a local beekeeper or your local authority.

• • • •

If you have bees in a chimney, light a fire in the grate and this should remove them safely and harmlessly. Some bumblebees are endangered species.

# CATS

Save used tea bags and dry them, add a few drops of Olbas oil, citronella oil, or eucalyptus oil to each one, and spread them around the areas in your garden frequented by cats.

· · · ·

Provide an area for cats to use by turning over some dirt in a garden bed. Spray them with a hose or keep a spray bottle of water handy.

· · · ·

Sink a jam jar of ammonia in the cat-path or save urine and spray onto area.

· · · ·

Place a small length of hose pipe in among your plants; cats and birds don't like snakes!

· · · ·

If using grated soap to deter cats, it is best to use coal tar, or sprinkle curry powder or chilli pepper powder around the boundaries where they frequent.

· · · ·

Scatter mothballs on flower beds to deter cats from visiting your garden.

· · · ·

On gravel driveways, scatter small pieces of orange peel around the borders to keep cats away.

· · · ·

To deter cats from using your borders as a convenience, place the trimmings from your pruned roses between the plants.

. . . .

If there are rats or mice in a garden, cats can do more good than harm!

## EARWIGS

Earwigs feed at night and hide during the day under leaves or rubbish. Remove all debris that they can hide under.

. . . .

Fill pots loosely with straw and set these up on canes or poles to entrap them. Shake out the traps daily over a bowl of paraffin or insecticide.

## EELWORMS

There are different species of eelworm. Each one keeps to its specific plant (including weeds), and even if its host is removed, it can still remain in the soil in the form of a dormant cyst for three years or more.

. . . .

The stem and bulb eelworm causes stunted growth in a wide range of bulbous and herbaceous plants.

. . . .

Leaf eelworms attack many flowering plants; it is particularly destructive to chrysanthemums.

. . . .

Root eelworms can attack many vegetables and flowering plants. One species of these can attack potato tubers, resulting in little or no crop.

. . . .

The root-knot eelworms attack a wide variety of plant hosts— particularly cucumbers, tomatoes, and flowers grown under glass.

. . . .

There is no method of control that will eradicate the different species. Reducing infestation or preventing it progressing is the best solution.

. . . .

All weeds and rubbish must be removed, pots and seed boxes cleaned and sterilized, prepared seed and potting composts used, and soil in greenhouse borders must be sterilized or replaced from a tested source.

. . . .

All plants purchased should be from a reliable source.

. . . .

Susceptible crops must not be planted in infested soil for over four years. In a vegetable garden, a long rotation should be strictly followed.

# MICE

Use fruit and nut chocolate for bait instead of cheese.

• • • •

Bait can be placed in a milk bottle or similar jar, which should be placed on a ramp (with the neck higher than the base). The mouse can then go in to feed but will not be able to get back out. The captured mouse can then be allowed to go free in a more suitable area (well away from the house).

• • • •

Ensure any holes large enough to insert a ball pen in are filled, as mice can use these to enter the house.

• • • •

When trying to catch mice, site traps horizontally around the edge of the room. This will then be effective whichever way the mouse runs.

• • • •

If you don't know where the rodent is coming from, sprinkle flour on the floor around the area and it will then be evident from the footprints. A tray containing lard or solid fat can also do the trick.

• • • •

If mice have destroyed a row of newly sown peas, the peas used in subsequent sowings should be coated in a mixture of paraffin and red lead made to a consistency of cream.

*"A good gardener always plants three seeds—*
*one for the bugs, one for the weather, and one for himself."*
*—Leo Aikman*

## MILLIPEDES

These must not be confused with centipedes, which are beneficial
to the garden as they feed on various insects.

. . . .

Millipedes have two pairs of legs and curl up when disturbed.

. . . .

Millipedes are from ½"–1" (1–2 cm) long, with a flat body.
According to the species, they can be black with white legs, or
yellowish-white to dull brown.

. . . .

They feed on a variety of vegetable matter and often feed on
tissue already damaged.

. . . .

Eradication is virtually impossible, but good general hygiene and
cultivation keeps them at bay.

. . . .

If there is a large infestation of millipedes, they can be trapped
by placing pieces of carrot or potato just under soil level. Check
every few days and remove and destroy.

## MOLES

If there is a problem with moles in the garden, find the run and place a small piece of gorse in the bottom. The prickles on the gorse will stop them returning. Alternatively, a child's "windmill" (the sort you get at the seaside) poked into the ground above the run causes vibrations that deters moles.

## MOSQUITOES, GNATS, AND MIDGES

Females feed on blood, biting mostly at dusk. Eggs are laid in stagnant water. Clean out guttering, birdbaths, rain barrels, etc. as these are ideal breeding sites.

• • • •

Doors and windows can be screened and repellents can be used on skin.

## PEA MOTHS

This small grayish-brown moth appears from mid-June to mid-August over the peas that are in flower or in pods. The caterpillars eat into the pods and cause damage.

• • • •

Damage can be curtailed by sowing early and late crops and avoiding the midseason. Regularly hoe between the rows to destroy the larvae.

## RABBITS

The only secure method is to enclose the garden with 1" (2.5 cm) mesh wire netting, 3' (1 m) high and sunk 18" (50 cm) below ground level.

• • • •

*"What is a weed?*
*A plant whose virtues have not yet been discovered."*
*—Ralph Waldo Emerson*

A line of fish manure spread around the boundaries of the garden can act as a repellent, but it must be renewed after heavy rain.

• • • •

Pour vinegar into a wide-necked jar and soak corn cobs (cut in half) in it for five minutes, then scatter around the vegetable or flower garden. Reuse the vinegar every two weeks.

• • • •

Use red pepper, black pepper, cayenne, or paprika as a dust to repel rabbits, as they are always sniffing.

• • • •

Mix a well beaten egg, ½ tsp (2 ml) Tabasco sauce, and 1 gal (5 ltr) water. Paint on tree trunks to prevent munching. It will not harm the trees.

• • • •

Make a solution of cow manure and water to spray on the garden.

## SLUGS AND SNAILS

Bury empty shallow cans or empty grapefruit halves in the soil so that the top is level with the ground, fill the can or grapefruit with beer, and the slugs crawl in, drink, and die.

• • • •

Bake eggshells in an oven to harden and then place around plants to prevent slugs damaging them. The slugs cannot get over the hardened shells. Or completely encircle the base of the plant with washed, roughly crushed eggshells. Ash and grit can also be effective.

. . . .

Sprinkle slugs with salt to kill them.

. . . .

Vaseline smeared around plant pots stops slugs getting to the plants inside.

. . . .

Make a slug catcher by using a 1 ltr plastic drink bottle. Cut the bottle two thirds of the way up all the way around, making two pieces. Cut around the neck of the bottle and discard the neck. Invert the section of bottle that is left to form a funnel inside the other part and staple together if necessary. Put about 2" (5 cm) of water into the bottle along with a few slug pellets. This should be sunk in the flower bed so that the top is level with the soil. The idea is that the slugs and snails climb into the bottle, but as the slug pellets are contained within the bottle they are not harmful to birds and animals that come into the garden.

. . . .

To prevent slugs and snails from attacking your plants, place a handful of bran in the bottom of a terra-cotta flowerpot and lay the pot on its side to distract them from your plants.

. . . .

To deter slugs from crawling up into flowerpots on a patio, wind some copper wire just under the rim (or a little lower) around the pot—it will give them a little electric shock.

## WASPS

Wasps are at their worst during August and September but die naturally by the end of autumn. They're attracted to sweet food and drinks.

. . . .

Stay still and they will soon go away. If you try to swat them, their friends may come and help.

. . . .

Trap with jars partly filled with water, jam, and a drop of liquid dish soap, covered with a punctured paper lid. Individual wasps can be destroyed by a proprietary wasp or fly killer.

. . . .

Seek advice from an environmental health department or pest control company before tackling wasp nests.

## WEEVILS

Weevils are a type of beetle with a snoutlike head and no legs.

. . . .

Weevils vary in color, some with a sheen, stripes, or bands. They are mostly gray or brown to black and about ½" (1.25 cm) long.

. . . .

*"Man is by definition the first and primary weed under whose influence all other weeds have evolved."*
—Jack R. Harland

Hiding by day and feeding at night, they eat the tissues of many trees, bushes, and plants.

• • • •

The adults can be trapped in pieces of sacking or corrugated paper while the grubs may be picked off the roots of pot plants. The plants should be repotted in fresh sterilized soil with an insecticide added.

## WIREWORMS

Wireworms are slow-moving, shiny, yellowish-brown grubs common in most soils, especially newly broken up turf.

• • • •

They are larvae of the click beetles which are brown to black, ½" (1.25 cm) long, and click when disturbed. The larvae vary in length.

• • • •

They feed on roots and stems of most plants and burrow into bulbs, potatoes, and other root crops.

• • • •

They do not affect the growth of established plants, but seedlings or young plants may wilt and die. If there is a large infestation, they can be trapped like the millipedes.

## INSECTICIDES

Before using any homemade spray, always pretest on a small area of the plant to make sure it will not harm it.

. . . .

To control aphids: chop up a few garlic gloves, one large onion, and a few chive leaves and place in a blender. Fill the blender half full with water. After blending the ingredients well, strain to form a clear solution and discard the pulp. Add additional water to make 1 gal (5 ltr) of spray. When using on plants, make sure to spray the undersides of the leaves where the aphids hide. This spray will kill the aphids but not harm other beneficial insects. It also helps to control whiteflies.

. . . .

For organic insecticide spray, boil a whole bulb of chopped garlic until it's soft. Put it into 1 gal (5 ltr) water and add 1 tbsp of biodegradable detergent. Leave for a day, strain, and use as required.

. . . .

Garlic spray for wire-worm, slugs, caterpillars, and weevils: chop 3 oz (75 g) garlic and mix with 2 tsp mineral oil. Leave for twenty-four hours then add 1 pt (500 ml) water with 2 tsp dissolved soap added. Stir well and strain into a plastic container. To use, dissolve one part of the mixture with twenty parts water and spray onto the leaves of affected vegetables and the surrounding soil.

. . . .

Insect repellent spray: mix together garlic, onion, lavender leaves or flowers, yarrow, and mint with just enough water to mix. Leave standing at room temperature for twenty-four hours in a closed container. Strain and add a few drops of detergent to help its ability to stick to the plants. Then add equal quantity of water and spray as required.

. . . .

Rhubarb aphids spray: chop six to seven green leaves of rhubarb and boil in 4 pt (2 ltr) water for thirty minutes. Strain and cool. Add a few flakes of soft soap and use as required.

. . . .

Tobacco spray for aphids, bugs, and small caterpillars: take 5 g of tobacco (approx. one to two large pinches) and pour over 2 pt (1 ltr) boiling water and let boil for 15 minutes or until the brew looks the strength of weak tea. Let it cool and strain. It is best to use this fresh, but it can be kept for a few days.

. . . .

Repellent for cucumber beetles: mix a handful of wood ash with a handful of hydrated lime and 2 gal (10 ltr) water. Mix well, then with a spray bottle, spray both sides of your cucumber leaves.

. . . .

To get rid of powdery mildew from cucumber or strawberry plants, mix 0.2 oz (6 g) baking soda (bicarbonate of soda) with 1 gal (5 ltr) water. Using a spray bottle, spray on leaves weekly to rid the plants of mildew.

. . . .

Instead of using chemicals on mildewed plants, make a solution of 90 percent water and 10 percent fresh milk and spray it onto the plant. Enzymes in the milk will attack the mildew. Don't go over 30 percent milk or you may end up with foul-smelling plants.

. . . .

Spray milk on apples and lettuce to control mildew. For large areas, dilute one part milk in nine parts water.

. . . .

To kill weeds without using harmful chemicals, fill a spray bottle with vinegar and zap the weeds with it. Just make sure not to spray your nearby crops. This will work on weed seedlings as well as full-grown plants. For particularly tough weeds, use cider vinegar, which has a higher acidity.

. . . .

To help weed easily between slabs or crazy paving, pour on the slightly salted boiling water after cooking potatoes. Even dandelions soon go after a couple of treatments.

. . . .

To rid roses of black spot disease, mix 1 tbsp baking soda, 1 tbsp vegetable oil, and 1 tbsp liquid dish soap in 1 gal (5 ltr) water and spray on the roses once a week.

# WEED CONTROL

Although it is best to prevent weed seeds from germinating or becoming established in the garden, sometimes it will be necessary to deal with them.

. . . .

Use opaque plastic sheeting to warm the soil for heat-loving tomatoes, peppers, and strawberries. The plastic absorbs heat during the day and keeps the soil warm at night. This is especially helpful during cool spring weather. The plastic also smothers the weeds between the rows and reduces evaporation from the soil beneath. Thick black plastic sheets can be used and these can usually be reused the following season. Before planting peppers, tomatoes, or strawberries, lay the plastic on the ground where the plants will grow. Cut 6" (15 cm) holes in the plastic every 2' (50 cm). Dig a hole for each transplant where there is a hole in the plastic, add organic matter, and plant. Be sure there is enough plastic on all sides to fully cover a mature root system. If using drip irrigation in the garden, put the drip lines under the plastic. If using sprinklers, dampen the soil before laying down the plastic and cut the holes larger to ensure that enough moisture enters the ground from the sprinklers. After everything is planted, weigh down the edges of the plastic with rocks or a few mounds of soil. Throughout the summer, the plastic will help control weeds, reduce moisture loss, and help to ripen warm-weather fruits and vegetables. By leaving the plastic in place over the winter, the soil will be weed-free and easy to work come planting time the next spring. Note that the plastic gives slugs and snails a place to hide.

. . . .

Regular hoeing and hand weeding can control most weeds. Hoeing is a very effective method of dealing with annual weeds. Hoe as soon as you see the weeds surfacing above the soil. Push the hoe just below the soil level to sever the weeds. Try to hoe when the ground is dry so weed seeds brought to the surface will not germinate.

• • • •

There are garden tools now available that are specially made for removing weeds. Choose one that removes the greatest amount of root system and the least amount of surrounding soil.

• • • •

Perennial weeds are best dug up, as they are difficult to control by other methods. Perennial weeds tend to spread by their creeping stems or roots and fragments of root. Ensure that all the roots are dug up or they will return.

• • • •

Planting ground covering plants will cut down the amount of weeding. However, before planting, all perennial weeds need to be removed. Having groundcover doesn't mean you will always have a weed-free area, but it will be easier to maintain.

• • • •

Mulching can suppress annual weeds and conserve soil moisture. Perennial weeds will still come through the mulch, so they need to be dug out by the roots. Use well-rotted compost and grass cuttings, providing the lawn they came from is weed free, or use decomposed wood chips.

• • • •

To help prevent the spread of disease, destroy diseased plants. Try to remove infected plants as soon as you notice them. Otherwise, the disease might spread to nearby plants. It usually is easier to spot disease problems in trees and shrubs in the summer or autumn when leaves are present. Avoid composting diseased plants, including fallen leaves from diseased trees or shrubs, since several disease-causing organisms can survive in compost.

. . . .

When removing diseased branches, prune 2"–3" (5–7 cm) below the infected area. If you do cut into the infected part of the limb, sterilize your pruning equipment by wiping the blades with rubbing alcohol or a mixture of one part household bleach and nine parts water.

. . . .

Clean and prepare garden beds in winter to have them ready for the spring. Dig in, compost, or remove and destroy crop refuse soon after you finish harvesting your garden.

. . . .

Removing plant refuse eliminates places where disease-causing organisms can overwinter.

. . . .

When using chemical weed killer, always carefully read the instructions on the product to ensure that you have the correct product for the task.

. . . .

Never store garden chemicals outdoors. Place large bags on a rack to allow air to circulate beneath.

. . . .

Never mix two different types of garden chemicals unless the manufacturers specifically state on the instructions that this can be done.

. . . .

Do not spray any garden chemical on a windy day or in frosty weather. Adjust the nozzle on the garden sprayer so that the spray is just a fine mist.

. . . .

Always clearly mark any watering cans or sprayers used for weed killer. Do not use these for watering or for applying other garden chemicals.

. . . .

Contact-acting insecticides and fungicides only work if they make contact with the organisms. Systemic-acting types are taken up into the sap and spread throughout the plant.

. . . .

If a lawn is treated with weed killer, the grass cuttings should not be put in the compost for six months.

# Garden Tools

*"Lawn mower: a magic wand for making*
*teenagers disappear."*
—Michael Garofalo

If plastic garden furniture is stained, make a paste of baking soda and water, apply it for a few minutes, then wipe off.

. . . .

To preserve aluminium garden furniture and metal tools over the winter, apply oil (either cooking oil or motor oil). Wipe off before using again, though.

. . . .

Paint the handles of gardening tools with leftover paint—the brighter the better—to make them easier seen in the garden.

. . . .

Clay soil can be difficult to dig; sharpen the end of the spade with a file to make it easier.

. . . .

Use an old fanny pack to keep secateurs, plant labels, string, a penknife, and other garden tools nearby. The expanding waist strap will enable it to go comfortably over bulky jackets and jumpers.

. . . .

Wrap a long length of string to one handle of secateurs and a few elastic bands to the other handle; they always come in handy in the garden.

. . . .

Keep an old oily rag in the garden shed for wiping tools after use, especially at damp times of the year. It will help keep them rust-free and clean.

. . . .

To avoid getting kinks in a garden hose, coil in a figure eight, not a circle.

. . . .

An old wheel rim makes an ideal storage place for a garden hose when not in use. Hang on a garage or shed wall.

. . . .

If the handles of tools, mowers, or shears are uncomfortable to hold, buy a foam bicycle handlebar grip. Slip the grips over the tool handles, using liquid dish soap or Vaseline if it proves difficult. Or slit the grip and slip it over the handle. Pipe insulating foam could also be used.

. . . .

If the hose springs a leak, make a temporary repair by inserting a cocktail stick into the hole. Snap the stick off as close to the hose as possible and wrap around with insulating tape or waterproof tape. This should extend by about 2" (5 cm) on each side of the hole. As the wood absorbs the water it will expand and seal the hole.

# TOOLS

Always buy strong, good-quality tools and look after them well. If you can afford it, buy stainless steel as they will last a lifetime and are easier to clean.

. . . .

When choosing tools, handle them before buying to make sure they feel good in your hand, and try out for balance and weight. With shovels and spades, check the length of the handle for comfort.

. . . .

*SHOVELS:* Round-pointed shovels are strictly for digging. The long-handled version works well for light-duty, stand-up digging, while a short-handled shovel is better for deep digging. A flat-ended shovel doesn't work well for digging, but it's perfect for things like scooping compost and cutting borders. Half-moon shovels or spades work well for keeping borders tidy and straight.

. . . .

*RAKES:* A wider-than-usual grading rake with teeth made from nearly indestructible nylon is ideal for leveling newly prepared ground or for drawing down the length of raised beds. Rakes with metal tines tend to last longest. They also can make the job easier because the teeth don't bend when they hit a heavy patch of leaves.

. . . .

*PITCHFORKS:* Square-tine versions are much stronger and can take a good deal of punishment. Use a pitchfork to loosen the subsoil in beds by simply driving it into the soil and gently rocking back and forth.

. . . .

*PRUNING SHEARS OR SHARP SECATEURS:* A good pair of hand clippers used for trimming rosebushes and shrubs.

. . . .

*LOPPERS:* This long-handled cutting tool is versatile enough to use for trimming rosebushes or cutting through branches about 1" (2.5 cm) in diameter. Useful in areas hard to reach with clippers or small shears.

. . . .

*HEDGE SHEARS:* Long-handled, flat-bladed hedge shears designed to cut evenly across a plane, either horizontal or vertical. Unless you have a large amount of greenery, hand hedge shears will work just as well as electric shears.

. . . .

*TANK SPRAYER:* Very useful for pest or weed control or for fertilizing an area. There are 1 gal (5 ltr) sprayers for smaller yards, and wheeled multi-gallon sprayers for larger areas.

. . . .

*GARDEN HOSE:* The length should be determined by the size of the garden. Too long a hose will become a tangled mess, while too short a hose is a nuisance. A rack or reel to keep the hose in good shape helps eliminate kinks that can impede flow already compromised by low water pressure in some areas and to make storage convenient when the hose isn't in use. A more expensive hose usually is better able to survive a hot summer and freezing winter temperatures. Check if the hose is made from material that is safe for drinking water.

. . . .

*WHEELBARROW:* A wheelbarrow can be used for a variety of gardening activities from moving dirt for a new plant bed to mixing concrete for a patio fix. If all you plan to do is move leaves, plastic wheelbarrows weigh less.

· · · ·

*SPREADER:* These help to spread fertilizer more evenly over the garden.

· · · ·

*A SQUARE-ENDED SPADE* is for digging large holes and double-digging.

· · · ·

*A HOE* is for weeding, cultivating, and opening seed furrows.

· · · ·

*A TROWEL* (or a large kitchen spoon) is for transplanting and applying dry fertilizers.

· · · ·

*A WATERING CAN* and maybe a sprinkler system are very helpful to have.

. . . .

*A FILE*, sharpening stone, or diamond file keeps tools sharp.

. . . .

*OTHERS:* A pruning saw, lawn mower, cotton gloves, and a hat will serve you well.

. . . .

Wipe tools with an oily rag before putting them away to keep them in good order for next time.

. . . .

Keep hand shears in a sturdy leather sheath that easily fits on a belt. This will not only keep them handy, but it will prevent them from poking holes through pockets.

## SHARPENING GARDEN TOOLS

Since gardening tools are expensive, it pays to take care of them properly. The best way to ensure that your tools will last a long time is to give them a thorough once-over before you put them away for the winter.

. . . .

Keep a small garden trowel working smoothly by regularly sharpening the edge with a file.

. . . .

Shovels, trowels, hoes, pruning shears, and hedge clippers will all work better if sharpened regularly.

. . . .

Before starting, clean all rust off the tools to be sharpened.

. . . .

Always wear safety goggles and leather gloves when filing or sharpening metal.

. . . .

Cut up some sandpaper to sharpen pruning shears. Use a 320-grit wet or dry sandpaper and cut three to four strips of sandpaper. Do this once a week for shears that are used frequently, and put a drop of lubricant on the pivot screw to keep the shears working smoothly. This method also works for sharpening scissors.

. . . .

On a hedge clipper, first clean the blades with a piece of steel wool and make sure none of the blades are bent. If a blade is bent, loosen the pivot nut and separate the blades, put the bent blade in a vice, and tweak it until it is straight.

. . . .

Once the blades are straight, clamp one blade in the vice with the blade side facing up. Examine the factory edge, hold the file with both hands, and follow the direction of the bevel. Move the file in one broad stroke, moving away, along the entire cutting area. Apply moderate pressure on the downward side of the coarse metal file, going across the blade. Repeat this motion several times until the whole edge shows an even line of exposed, clean metal. This can take up to ten strokes. Repeat the process on the other blade.

. . . .

Remove burrs from the blade by placing a sheet of 300-grit wet or dry sandpaper on a smooth, flat piece of plywood. Lightly sand the backside of the blade using a circular motion. After several circles, check to see if the burrs are gone. Reassemble the hedge clippers and cut away.

· · · ·

Use a file to remove nicks and smooth the edges of shovels and trowels. Before beginning, clean the trowel or shovel thoroughly with steel wool. Coat with a silicone spray for a finishing touch. This prevents rust and keeps soil from sticking to the tool.

· · · ·

Sharpen a garden hoe by filing the inside edge first, working away from the handle. Then take the feathered edge off the outside surface. A sharp hoe cuts through the ground with ease.

· · · ·

Clean all metal surfaces to remove any dirt that can harbor moisture and cause the metal to rust. Small and large stiff wire brushes work best for this task.

· · · ·

Once all the dirt has been removed, soak a cloth in motor oil, WD-40, or vegetable oil and coat the metal surfaces thoroughly. The oil coating will prevent rust from forming on the metal should moisture find its way into your garage or toolshed.

· · · ·

Wooden tool handles should be treated to prevent drying and cracking that can lead to splinters. Soak a rag in boiled linseed oil and rub the handle, allowing it to absorb the oil. Check to see that any screws or bolts are fastened securely.

. . . .

Clean resinous sap from the metal surfaces of loppers or secateurs/pruners with a cloth soaked in methalyted spirit, turpentine, or warm soapy water, then file the cutting edge.

. . . .

Oil pivot points with a light household oil or WD-40. A honing stone should be used to sharpen these tools, but the technique is difficult, so it is better to get an authorized service agent to sharpen high-quality shears or secateurs.

. . . .

Clean your gardening tools throughout the growing season, rather than waiting until the end of the year to do it. Get a good-sized barrel or bucket, fill it with sand, and add a quart of motor oil, then each time you use your tool, stab it a few times in the sand. The grit of the sand will knock the dirt off the metal surfaces and the oil will put a nice shine on the tool and keep it from rusting.

. . . .

A regular garden hose pumps out 20 gal of water per minute. If left on for 24 hours, that's 28,800 gal Better not forget to turn it off!

## LAWN MOWERS

Before putting your lawn mower away for the winter, give it a thorough cleaning and checkup.

. . . .

Disconnect electric cables from sockets or spark plugs and battery cable and remove caked-on grass and mud from around the blades.

. . . .

To prevent rusting when not in use, wipe all moving parts with a lightly oiled rag.

. . . .

Lubricate all moving parts; spray rust inhibitor on the blade and other unpainted metal parts.

. . . .

Check if the blades and cutters need sharpening, tightening, or even replacing.

. . . .

Examine electric mower cables and any with signs of damage or badly worn should be replaced immediately.

. . . .

If you have a motor mower, drain the gas and oil tanks and clean the spark plug. Fill oil tank with clean oil but leave the gas tank empty as gas deteriorates.

. . . .

Get replacement parts or repairs done before storing for the winter as it is more difficult to get them done in the springtime.

. . . .

Lightly sand and paint any rusted or peeling spots on the mower's metal body.

. . . .

Never leave a motor mower standing for months on a damp surface or in a damp place as this will inevitably make it difficult to start in spring. Stand it on a piece of cardboard or a block of wood and keep the area as well ventilated as possible to avoid condensation.

• • • •

If the mower refuses to start, take out the plug and dip the sparking end in gas, replace, connect, and the mower should start.

## SAFETY TIPS WHEN USING LAWN MOWERS

Fill a gas-fueled mower outdoors and keep away from cigarettes or other heat sources. Wipe up any spills and replace the gas cap immediately, securing tightly.

• • • •

Do not turn gas mower on its side to inspect underneath as it will result in the gas and/or oil leaking out.

• • • •

If the blades of a lawn mower need to be examined or get clogged with wet grass, switch off the engine and disconnect the spark plug before examining the blades or removing the grass.

• • • •

Make sure that electric mowers are fitted with a circuit breaker. This will prevent any nasty accident should it come into contact with moisture or the cable is damaged in any way.

• • • •

*"The grass may be greener on the other side of the fence,
but you still have to mow it." —Unknown*

Cables should run behind electric lawn mowers; never cut toward
a flex, or use it in wet conditions.

• • • •

Never clean or adjust electrical gardening equipment while they
are still plugged in; make sure they are switched off first.

• • • •

Never wash electrical gardening equipment with water.

• • • •

Before mowing, clear the lawn of any debris, as this can be picked
up and spun out by the blades, causing accidents.

• • • •

Never run a mower over gravel.

• • • •

Wear heavy shoes or boots when mowing. Avoid loose clothing,
jewelery, and sandals. Tie long hair back.

• • • •

Mow across a slope rather than up and down. You will have better
control of the mower and will be less likely to fall toward the mower.

• • • •

Turn the engine off when leaving it unattended, however quick
you intend to be. Never allow children to use a lawn mower.

# Healthy Gardening

*"Have patience. All things change in due time.*
*Wishing cannot bring autumn glory*
*or cause winter to cease."*
*—Ginaly-li*

## GARDEN TIPS

If you hate wearing gardening gloves, rub petroleum jelly
into your hands and push it well under the fingernails before
gardening; it'll make hand cleaning much easier. Or scrape nails
over a bar of soap and they will be easier cleaned.

. . . .

To clean hands after gardening, put a little olive oil and a little
sugar on the hands and rub well into the skin. Remove with warm,
soapy water.

. . . .

To remove a splinter from your finger, put a little damp sugar
over the affected area and cover with a Band-Aid. After a few days
the skin will have softened and the splinter can be easily forced
to the surface.

. . . .

Always wear gloves when handling bonemeal, especially if you
have cuts on your hands.

. . . .

The sap of the poinsettia is an irritant; always remember to wash
hands after handling.

. . . .

Rub vanilla extract on skin to repel gnats.

. . . .

Always wear goggles when using hedge trimmers, string cutters, chain saws, or garden shredders.

. . . .

Only store garden chemicals in their original packaging. Keep in a secure place out of reach of children or animals.

## GARDENING WARM-UPS

These stretches prepare for the lifts, bends, and pulls common to working in the garden.

. . . .

Upper Body Twist: Stand with hands on hips. Slowly turn upper body as far as possible to the left for a count of five. Turn to the right for a count of five. Repeat ten times.

. . . .

Upper Body Stretch: Stand with back straight and arms at your sides. Stretch arms straight out in front of you and hold for a count of five. Return arms to sides. Repeat ten times.

. . . .

Now, stretch arms back until shoulder blades touch. Hold for a count of five. Return arms to sides. Repeat ten times.

## HEALTHY GARDENING

Gardening is a popular leisure activity for many people, but it can be difficult if a person has health conditions that limit movement or stamina. Even among fit people, gardening can take a greater physical toll than necessary. The solution lies in garden planning and layout, lifting, and ergonomic tools, adapting the work or tool to the individual rather than vice versa.

## PLANNING

Be aware of your own physical limitations. Plan your tasks and organize the tools you will need before you start. Break the task down and take rest breaks.

. . . .

Before going into the garden, take an extra ten minutes to warm up the muscles with stretches and warm-up exercises.

. . . .

*"Gardening gives me fun and health and knowledge.*
*It gives me laughter and color.*
*It gives me pictures of almost incredible beauty."*
*—John F. Kenyon*

Lifting with your legs, not your back, can help prevent injury.

. . . .

It is important to position yourself so that muscles can be used for maximum efficiency. Maintaining an upright posture rather than continually reaching forward is a safer and more efficient use of muscles.

. . . .

Joints shouldn't be locked when standing. Sitting in a squatting position can be hard on the joints and difficult to get up from.

. . . .

Regarding arms, the straighter the elbow and the farther away it is from the body, the less efficient the position.

. . . .

Change position and tasks frequently and don't spend hours pruning or digging.

## SENSIBLE GARDEN PLANNING

Start with a small garden area that can be managed without excess exertion. It should be located near the house and the water supply to reduce hauling long lengths of hose.

. . . .

If possible, the garden area, tool storage, and work surfaces and watering sources should be close together.

. . . .

Consider putting in extra garden seating.

. . . .

Paths should be placed in the most direct route. Narrow pathways, steps, and uneven paved surfaces can create dangerous and inconvenient access problems.

. . . .

Gravel paths require constant maintenance and can be difficult and dangerous to walk on. Nonslip, hard, flat paving can be used without detracting from the appearance of the garden.

. . . .

Make garden paths wide enough so that all the heavy stuff can be hauled by a four-wheeled cart or a wheelbarrow instead of by you.

. . . .

Incorporate some back-friendly principles into your garden design. Raised beds and trellises are easier to maintain than in-ground beds.

. . . .

Limit bed depth to no more than twice the distance you can reach without straining.

. . . .

*"The love of gardening is a seed once sown
that never dies."*
*— Gertrude Jekyll*

To reduce water hauling, set up a rain barrel or hose near the garden; water weighs more than 8 lb (4 kg) per gallon. Or install an automated drip or soaker hose watering system.

## SMART DIGGING AND LIFTING

Keep your back straight when digging. When ready to plunge your shovel into the soil, remember that your spine is weaker if it's twisted, so face your shovel as you work and avoid digging in such a way that your back could be jerked to one side.

· · · ·

The way you use your shovel makes a difference to your back. Keep the blade vertical as you insert it into the soil for better leverage when you pull back on the handle.

· · · ·

If you have to lift, reduce the load. It is better to lift a shovel more times with less soil than fewer times with a heavy load each time. You'll get more aerobic benefit and less back strain.

· · · ·

Buying garden products in extra-large bags may mean savings in the pocket but not for the back. Even lifting 25 lb (10 kg) can cause injury, especially if you hold the bag low or far out in front. Choose bags with handles if possible, and lift with bent knees and a straight back. Rather than moving the whole bag, divide it into smaller, more manageable loads.

· · · ·

Set heavy objects that you'll need to lift again on a table instead of the ground. Use a garden cart or trolley to move heavy bags and containers around.

. . . .

To drag a heavy bag for a short distance, face it with bent knees and a straight back and pull it while straightening your legs.

## FRIENDLY TOOLS

As you work, keep your wrist as close as possible to its neutral position, that is, the position it's in when you're not using your hand. If your wrist is bent in any other direction, you have less strength and are more prone to injury.

. . . .

A wrist support in the form of a splint or brace prevents the wrist from bending without inhibiting finger movement.

. . . .

Wider handles 1½" (3.5 cm) in diameter reduce hand strain. Similarly, cushion textured grips require less effort to hold, and reduce or eliminate blisters. Wrap your thumb around the tool handle to avoid the strain of positioning it along the handle.

. . . .

It is important to vary your hand motions, take frequent breaks, and stop at the first sign of pain.

. . . .

There are a large selection of ergonomically designed garden tools now available, so choose well-designed tools and learn the best position for a tool-task combination.

. . . .

When it comes to long-handled tools, the longer the handle, the better (when you're standing). The less you bend, the less chance of back strain or injury. Long-handled tools with bent handles allow you to work without bending.

. . . .

Slip pistol-grip handles or spongy tubes onto the end of the handles of rakes, hoes, and hand tools to make them more comfortable for hands and backs.

. . . .

Whenever possible, keep a stool or small folding chair in the garden to rest on or to sit down while working. A garden kneeler has a kneeling pad and side handles for getting up and down. It can be turned upside down for use as a stool.

. . . .

If you must kneel, use cushioned strap-on knee pads or pants with padded knees.

. . . .

Use the ball of your foot, not the instep, to push a spade into the ground. Wear leather boots rather than Wellingtons when digging.

. . . .

Make your own planting devices. Polyvinyl chloride (PVC) pipe 2"–3" (5–7 cm) in diameter can be cut to 3'–4' (1–1½ m) in length, depending on how tall the user is. Sharpen one end so it can be used to draw a furrow in soil prepared for planting. Drop seeds at regular intervals through the pipe to provide the seed spacing. Turn over the pipe and drag it over the soil to fill the furrow.

· · · ·

Grow crops that can be managed without stooping as much. For example, small fruits such as blueberries and raspberries, vines, roses, and other perennials can often be cared for without stooping all the way over.

· · · ·

Avoid numerous trips. Make carrying easier with a sturdy box or basket with a handle to collect and hold seeds, plants, and tools, etc.

· · · ·

Combination tool systems are available with interchangeable tool heads and handles of varying lengths and weights. Some tools are designed for more than one action or use, which reduces the number of tools you need to carry around.

· · · ·

Lawn mowers can be heavy and difficult to use. Mowers with an electric starter cause less frustration and are easier on your back. A self-propelling mower will help to prevent back strain. Electric mowers suit some people, but need to be operated methodically to avoid problems with the power cord, and some users may find the swinging motion difficult to manage. Battery-operated mowers tend to create less noise and vibration.

· · · ·

Wheelbarrows are useful for gathering rubbish or moving heavy items around the garden. Wheelbarrows with two wheels rather than one are usually easier to use and the load is taken over the wheels rather than through the handles.

## HOW TO AVOID OTHER DANGERS

Always secure a ladder to a branch or other support if using it to cut a high hedge.

· · · ·

Do not overstretch when doing work in a garden pond. Lay large planks or a strong ladder across the pond and work from these.

· · · ·

Only use chemicals specifically sold for use in a garden. Do not use farm chemicals as they require special handling and application procedures.

· · · ·

Laburnum and yew leaves can be poisonous to eat, so it is advisable not to plant these in a garden where there are young children.

# GARDEN HINTS

When planting peas and beans, the rows should always run north and south. This makes sense, since the sun moves from east to west and gives the plants maximum sunshine.

. . . .

When planting your tomatoes, place two crumbled eggshells in the bottom of each hole. This is an excellent source of calcium (an insufficient amount of calcium can cause blossom end rot). Also use crumbled eggshells around the base of plants to protect them from cut worms.

. . . .

Store gingerroot in the soil of a potted basil plant. The ginger helps the basil plant flourish.

. . . .

To harvest and cure onions properly, wait until 75 percent of the tops have fallen over naturally before harvesting the crop. Store them in a dry, shady place with good ventilation, such as an outdoor shed or barn, for ten days to two weeks. After the onions have cured, put them in slatted crates or mesh bags. Store them indoors in a cellar with low humidity and temperatures between 33°F/3°C and 45°F/7°C.

. . . .

Put 1–2 tbsp Epsom salts in the hole before placing the tomato plant. Then cover with soil and water as usual. The use of Epsom salt is thought to add magnesium to the soil and help prevent blossom end rot. Generally, tomatoes tend to be heavy users of magnesium.

. . . .

Before filling a strawberry barrel with compost, stand a piece of drainpipe or cardboard tube upright in the center and fill with pebbles. As you fill with compost, gradually remove the tube releasing the pebbles. This will act as a central drainage system preventing the soil from becoming waterlogged.

• • • •

Sow seeds when it's dry; set plants when it's wet. If soil stays in a moist ball when squeezed hard, it is still too wet to plant seeds. Wait until the soil crumbles.

• • • •

Weed after a rainfall as weeds pull easier. If you need to weed and it hasn't rained, water your garden first.

# Glossary of Gardening Terms

*ACID SOIL*: usually a peaty or sandy soil with a pH of less than 7.0 containing little or no lime.

*AERATE*: to loosen soil compaction by digging, hoeing, or forking.

*ALKALINE SOIL*: chalky or limestone soil with a pH over 7.0.

*ANNUAL*: any plant that grows from seed to flower and dies within a year.

*BEDDING PLANTS*: plants set out for temporary display mainly in spring and summer. They are removed at the end of their flowering season.

*BIENNIAL*: plants that have a two-year life cycle. Seeds germinate and leaves develop in the first year and the plant matures in the second year.

*BOLTING*: prematurely running to seed.

*BRASSICA*: vegetables belonging to the cabbage family, like cauliflower and broccoli.

*BULB*: the underground storage, swollen part of plants, holding food reserves to keep plants like daffodils going during the winter.

*BUSH*: a shrub with branches that does not grow more than 30" (75 cm) tall.

CATCH CROP: quick maturing crop grown in the short time between lifting one main crop and planting another.

COMPOST: partly decomposed vegetable matter used as a manure substitute.

CONIFER: evergreen trees bearing cones. Pine, fir, and spruce belong to this group.

CORM: like the bulb, but the stem is swollen for storage of plant food.

CUTTING: a piece of stem, root, leaf, or shoot cut from a plant and used for propagation.

DEADHEAD: removing faded or dead blooms to encourage a new crop.

DECIDUOUS: shrubs and trees that shed their leaves in autumn and remain dormant until the spring.

DIBBER: a piece of wood used to make holes for planting.

DIVISION: the splitting up of root or crown clumps for propagation.

DORMANT: term given to plants when active growth has visibly stopped as with deciduous trees or leafless living bulbs.

DOUBLE DIGGING: digging to the double depth of the spade.

DWARF: specially bred small versions of normal-sized plants.

EARTHING UP: drawing up soil around the stems of a plant.

EVERGREEN: plants that retain their leaves throughout the year.

FERTILIZER: a substance containing concentrated plant foods essential for growth.

FUNGICIDE: a substance used to prevent or destroy fungi.

GERMINATION: the first stages of seed growth when leaves or shoots appear.

GROWING ON: the care of plants being nurtured indoors or in a greenhouse until they mature.

HARDEN OFF: acclimatizing plants raised in a heated environment before they are planted out.

HALF HARDY: A plant that cannot tolerate frost but can be grown outdoors once the danger of frost has passed.

HARDY: plants that can be grown outdoors all year round.

HERBACEOUS: plants with nonwoody stems that usually die back every winter.

HERBICIDE: a substance used for killing weeds.

INSECTICIDE: a substance used for killing insects.

INTERCROP: a crop grown between rows of another vegetable.

LATERAL: a side shoot or growth developing from a main stem.

LOAM: fertile soil composed of a balanced mixture of sand, clay, and decayed organic matter.

MANURE: a mixture of animal and vegetable waste.

MULCH: a surface layer of organic matter, used to suppress weeds and conserve moisture.

ORGANIC GARDENING: a method where only organic manure and compost are used and the use of herbicides and pesticides are restricted.

PERENNIAL: nonwoody plants that live for many years but die back in winter.

*PINCHING OUT*: nipping off the growing point of a shoot or stem to encourage bushy growth or to hasten maturity.

*POLLINATION*: the transfer of pollen from one flower to another or from one part of a plant to another to give fertilization of fruit blossom and set seeds.

*POT-BOUND*: when roots of a container-grown plant have outgrown the pot.

*PRICKING OUT*: transplanting seedlings from where they were germinated to another container.

*PROPAGATION*: the reproduction of plants.

*PRUNING*: the systematic cutting out of unwanted shoots.

*ROOT BALL*: a mass of roots with compost or soil surrounding them.

*ROOTSTOCK*: the root part of a grafted or budded plant.

*RUNNER*: the above ground stem connecting a new plant to the parent plant.

*SCARIFY*: to aerate turf with a wire rake.

*SEED BED*: an area of ground prepared for seed growing.

*SEED LEAVES*: the first leaf or pair of leaves, after germination.

*SET*: a partly developed bulb specially treated and used instead of seed for crop production. Set when applied to fruit trees means the fertilization of the flower and the start of fruit development.

*SHRUB*: a woody plant with more than one main stem growing at or near ground level.

*SPIT*: the depth of a spade, about 10" (25 cm).

*SUCKER*: a growth or shoot arising below or near soil level.

*SYSTEMIC*: a fungicide, insecticide, or fertilizer that is able to penetrate the leaves and enter the sap system.

*TENDER*: the term applied to plants needing protection from frost or severe weather.

*TILTH*: the texture of soil.

*TOP DRESSING*: a surface application of plant food such as compost or fertilizer.

*TRANSPLANTING*: lifting plants and replanting in a new area or pot.

*TRUE LEAVES*: the leaves that appear after the seed leaves and are typical of the plant.

*TUBER*: a swollen, underground root or stem acting as a food store.

*VARIEGATED*: plants whose leaves or petals have two or more colors.

*WATERLOGGED*: the term applied to soil that is saturated with water, resulting in the absence of air between soil particles, which is essential for growth.

*WEED*: a plant usually of little value growing where it is not wanted.

# Index